Cycle Breakers

Cycle Breakers

Free Yourself from Emotionally Immature Parents and Be the Parent You Wish You'd Had

Harriet Shearsmith

Zeitgeist • New York

Zeitgeist™
An imprint and division of Penguin Random House LLC
1745 Broadway, New York, NY 10019
zeitgeistpublishing.com
penguinrandomhouse.com

Originally published in the United Kingdom as *Unfollowing Mum* by
Vermilion, an imprint of Ebury Publishing, a division of Penguin Random
House UK, in 2024.

ISBN: 9798217151479
Ebook ISBN: 9798217151462

Printed in the United States of America on acid-free paper
1st Printing

The authorized representative in the EU for product safety and compliance
is Penguin Random House Ireland, Morrison Chambers, 32 Nassau Street,
Dublin D02 YH68, Ireland. https://eu-contact.penguin.ie.

For my children—it is my greatest honor to be your mum.
May you break the cycles I don't and know you
always have a home in my heart.

Contents

A note from the author

Dear cycle breaker,

Before you jump in, I wanted to let you know a few things. Firstly, you probably grew up hearing phrases like "Just wait until you have kids and then you'll understand how hard it is" or "I hope you have a child just like you as payback." I want you to know that you were never hard to love, nor are you hard to love now, and it is my hope that through the lens of parenthood you will be able to see what a privilege it is to be a parent. That doesn't mean it's easy—especially if you have to contend with generational trauma and you're learning how to love yourself at the same time. Despite the challenges and pitfalls of being a parent, it is the greatest honor to be able to watch your child grow and develop into an adult, to guide them on their path. It's an honor and a privilege, but not something we're entitled to.

Which brings me to the second thing I would like you to know—no one is entitled to you just because they are titled to you. Not your time, your space or your joy.

In reading this book you're taking a step toward reparenting yourself and becoming the parent you wish you'd had growing up—someone who could focus on your needs, love you and respect you as an individual. Despite it all, you're choosing to be better, do better and challenge yourself. You're choosing to break cycles that span generations.

I'm really proud of you, of us.

Introduction

"Have you spoken to your mom?"

It's such a seemingly innocuous question, and yet for me it had the capability to snatch the breath from my lungs. The answer is simple, and to be expected after everything: no, I haven't spoken to my mom.

Three weeks prior to this conversation, my mom had moved out of the annex we had built for her and I hadn't spoken to her since. In fact, I hadn't spoken to her in months. Nearly four years later and I still haven't spoken to her.

It's incredibly difficult to explain to someone that you have no contact with a parent—give a little too much information and everyone is uncomfortable; give a blunt "we don't speak" and people feel compelled to slip into the uninvited (and deeply unqualified) role of family counselor or fixer. "Oh, but you only get one mom" is spewed at you, like you're not keenly aware that you only get one, and the one you got is so toxic that you've had to make the difficult choice to remove them from your life and, in a lot of cases, the lives of your children too. Yes, I know you only get one mom. As a parent myself, the phrase haunts me in a different way—I'm only too aware that the responsibility to be that "one mom" and do a decent enough job of it that my kids don't grow up to feel the way I do is on my shoulders. Shoulders that feel somewhat ill-equipped.

Where is my blueprint for what healthy parenthood should look like? Is it as simple as taking the way my parents parented and just doing the direct opposite? I wish. Every day as a mother I remember that I am the "only one" who can break the cycle of generational trauma for my three wonderful children. That the fact I would lay my life down for them without thought might not be enough to make me a "good parent," but without that having been modeled for me, I have no clue what a "good parent" looks like. While all of this speeds through my head at a gazillion miles an hour, I'm also trying to reparent myself and heal my childhood trauma, while challenging the conditioning I grew up with from my parents and wider society. Talk about pressure, huh? It feels like there are an infinite number of questions you could ask me that would be better than "Have you spoken to your mom?", and yet . . .

In this particular instance, I was just trying to collect my takeout food. We live in a small town, which means that takeout isn't available at the click of a button just yet. Actual human interaction, and occasionally a trip in the car, are required to secure the grub. Less hunter, but still very much gatherer. Living in a small town doesn't just pose the collection conundrum, it comes with the added complication that everyone knows everyone, which is exactly why the person who works at the takeout counter I've been visiting weekly for years asked me if I'd spoken to my mom. I'm still unsure exactly how they know each other. I think they worked in the same building at one point—so not close, but friendly enough for the odd chit-chat, and for her to become a fierce defender of

Mom's right to have a place in my life. We'd also had this conversation the week before, and the week before that.

The first week after Mom moved out the takeout woman (I don't know her name, because we don't know each other except for my weekly collections—but let us not allow that to stand in the way of personal questions and unsolicited advice) asked me how Mom was and I said, "Um, I haven't actually seen her for a while, but I hope she's well." In hindsight, I should have just said, "Fine." I was immediately met with, "What? What do you mean? You haven't seen her? Oh no, that's really shocked me, you were so close! Haven't you spoken on the phone? Can't you just call her? It's nearly Christmas!" It was my first real interaction post-estrangement with someone who knew my mom, and by proxy knew me, but didn't know that I'd cut her out of my life. I made some blustering excuse, hastily paid for the takeout and left. I'll admit my Friday night takeout is often the highlight of my week, a little pat on the back for surviving the mayhem, so when I didn't bustle through the door with a big smile, the children and my husband could sense that something had upset me.

"Are you OK, Mommy?" Shit. Another question that can scatter me. Sounds silly, doesn't it? After all, I want my kids to display empathy, but I don't want them to be responsible for my emotions. I want them to see that sadness and worry are normal, but I don't want to transfer my worries and fears, my pain, onto them—that's not very cycle breaking of me, is it? Growing up I felt I was my mother's stand-in spouse and therapist, while also frequently being reminded that I was *not* her friend and she was the grown-up . . . so which was it again? All these grown-up emotions—I remember sitting at the table while she talked about that day's court proceedings during my parents' divorce, or hearing about my dad's affairs and how they affected her—but I was not a friend or equal, just a child. Her child.

Now, when my children seek to comfort me, no matter how minorly, I'm launched back to those times when I was in that role as a child. Add to that the challenge that my children had a relationship with my mother up until they were five, seven and nine years old, so the estrangement was fresh for them too. I was still very much trapped in a toxic cycle with my mom when I had my first child at the age of 21, and I would go so far as to say that having them was the beginning of the end, as it so often is for most cycle breakers (even if that end doesn't mean an estrangement but a low-contact relationship or one with firm boundaries). I started to recognize that there was no way I would ever behave toward them the way my mother did toward me, and her behavior only became more difficult to cope with as I developed my own family and my own identity.

It took me just under a decade from starting to see the cracks in our relationship to it fully breaking down and ultimately ending in estrangement. Ten years to break away from a lifetime of conditioning, and no doubt I will spend a lifetime healing and relearning. So, with all of this in mind, I have always been keenly aware of how my reactions impact my children when the estrangement is mentioned. It all seems very unfair—in that moment I wanted to come home and have a good cry to my husband, but instead I plopped the takeout on the table and declared, "Nothing, my darling, the silly lady at the takeout counter said something that took me by surprise is all. Did you pick a movie? Oh, and could you grab knives and forks, please?" Nothing like a bit of distraction to save the day.

But by week three of this little dance, I was getting a bit fed up.

"Have you spoken to your mom?"

Deep breath. "No, I haven't, and I won't have next week either." The takeout woman looked a little affronted; she paused as she handed me the takeout. "I just think it's really sad, you only get one mom." Ahh, there it is. I smiled; I'd been prepared for something like this. "Yes," I said. "It is incredibly sad, but it's the best choice for me and it won't be changing anytime soon, so please don't ask me again." After that the takeout woman stopped asking me about Mom, and I've stopped trying to defend myself to people who I don't really care about, and whose opinions don't matter. I'm sure if you're reading this book, you have experienced the stranger-turned-mediator, and will know that they are nothing in comparison to family or close friends who dive into the fray when you choose to cut contact or distance yourself from a toxic parent, especially if you have children yourself.

Estrangement and low-contact relationships with parents don't just happen overnight or as a result of a singular incident—even if there is a catalyst for the decision. They're the culmination of years of "incidents" or behaviors that roll together to create the intolerable reality that this relationship is damaging and you can't continue allowing it to harm you. Since speaking out about my experience with estrangement, I have heard from thousands of people who have found themselves making the difficult decision to limit or end contact with a parent, yet not one of them has ever expressed to me that it was an easy decision based on an isolated incident, as many toxic family members and society would have us believe. It's a common misconception, aided by the notion that adult children who cut ties with their parents are just ungrateful or selfish. We are neither, but all too often this is the picture painted of us for enforcing boundaries to protect our mental and physical wellbeing, in a situation that has left us little other choice.

As Dr. Sherrie Campbell said in her book *Adult Survivors of Toxic Family Members: Tools to Maintain Boundaries, Deal with Criticism, and Heal from Shame After Ties Have Been Cut*, "Our larger society gives the message that you are cruel to set boundaries on those who raised you or on those whom you were raised with, especially when you set those boundaries on family as an adult." Cutting ties with a family member may seem cruel—it certainly seems extreme from an outsider's perspective—yet I wonder if it would seem extreme if the person you were cutting ties with wasn't a close relative offering you the same treatment? We'll look at this perception in more detail in chapter 6, but it's important to know that despite what you have been given to believe, you are not selfish, difficult or cruel for setting boundaries, including the ultimate boundary of ending the relationship. Making the choice, or considering it, doesn't make you wrong or cold-hearted. It is, however, a decision that will impact you for the rest of your life, and while you may make peace with it, as I have done, it will have a lasting impact, especially as you move into your own parenting journey.

Choosing myself and prioritizing my mental health has changed my life for the better, allowing me to discover who I am free from the toxic shadow that my relationship with my mother engulfed me, and everyone close to me, in. It has been liberating, but it has also been exhausting, and at times incredibly isolating. While the media and wider society love to shame adult children for being "cruel" and "ungrateful" when they make the choice to cut contact with or step back from a parent, especially a mother, they simultaneously love to idolize mothers and place them on an unrealistic pedestal that is detrimental to both child and parent. Not only does that set us up for "failure" by creating an unrealistic idea of what "should be" and is impossible for us to attain, but the impact is tenfold when you are parenting without a blueprint, consciously trying to avoid repeating the cycle and putting endless pressure on yourself to be the best parent so your children never feel the way you did. Parents are human and make mistakes, we know this to be true, but when society teaches us that they are exempt from accountability, you end up with a generational cycle of invalidation, trauma and resentment.

At some point, someone has to step up and break that cycle. That someone can be you, not just for future generations but for yourself too, though the question that so many of us find difficult to answer is *how*?

Well, let's explore that together throughout this book.

How to use this book

When I first started writing this book, I didn't realize quite how healing I would find it myself. As a certified coach and trainee therapist, I specialize in working with adult children who have either cut contact or are struggling to navigate a toxic family dynamic. I help them to heal their parent and inner child wounds and move forward into a happier and healthier future. It never occurred to me, even after working with countless clients over the years and building a community of cycle breakers who grew up in dysfunctional family dynamics, how cathartic it would be to create the very thing I needed when I started on this path.

Cycle breaking might mean different things to different people—it isn't a one-size-fits-all experience. Throughout this book we're going to look at what it means for you. Picking up this book might be the first step on your cycle-breaking journey, or perhaps you've been taking steps to break the cycle for yourself already and you want to dig a little deeper into how that looks for your parenting journey.

Maybe you've already got children and you've recognized some habits or behaviors you have that you'd rather leave behind, or you might be experiencing a breakdown in the relationship with your parent and you want to develop your self-awareness, build a foundation for your own parenting and better understand generational trauma (the passing down of behavioral patterns and trauma from generation to generation). You might be both! Regardless of where you're at, it is my hope that this book can support you through the process of self-discovery, learning and growth. Cycle-breaking parenting starts with you; you have to reparent yourself first, because we cannot break cycles while we're still trapped in them.

Throughout this book I'm going to invite you to join me on a journey with you at the center. We'll start by understanding what it might look like to grow up in a dysfunctional family dynamic, how that impacts us and how we can set boundaries with our family to protect ourselves. The aim of section 1 of the book is to help you understand that you're not just sensitive or dramatic, but that you and your feelings matter, and it's OK to acknowledge that what you experienced wasn't OK (even if you've come to a place where you have a really great relationship with your parent now!).

We'll talk about the stigma surrounding estrangement and the taboo of toxic family dynamics in section 2, what low-contact relationships with toxic parents might look like, and how to talk to your children about your experiences, the current state of your relationship with your parent and what that might mean for them.

In section 3 we will look at developing practical skills that can help you as you parent your own child. We'll take a deep dive into how our parenting can be affected by our childhood, and learn how to teach our children to set boundaries and how to be accountable when we mess up.

Finally, in section 4 we look at developing your self-awareness, learning what makes you tick and rediscovering who you are, not just as a parent, but as a person who perhaps hasn't been allowed to develop their own identity away from their family expectations.

Moving through the book, you will find lots of practical exercises; these are your "cycle breaker's toolkits." They are there to help you develop a set of skills to support you as you navigate the challenges of parenting without a blueprint. You'll be able to refer to these as often as you like, and use these skills to heal and grow wherever and whenever you need to.

At the back of the book is a collection of resources, including books, podcasts, websites, healing practices, therapy advice and even social media accounts that may be able to offer you further support on this road. I've done my best to curate as many useful resources as possible because I know first hand how challenging it can be to find them, how isolating it can feel to be a cycle breaker (especially when your family isn't supportive of your choices) and how powerful validation and community support can be. There is so much healing to be found and it brings me joy to think I can direct you toward it.

I strongly recommend you grab a blank journal to work in alongside this book, as you might find it helpful to jot down your thoughts and feelings as you put the work in. At the end of each section of the book you will find some guided journaling prompts and exercises. In addition to responding to the prompts, you might want to make a note of anything within the section that particularly stuck with you, or answer some of the questions I've posed in the preceding chapters. Whatever works for you—your journal is your space.

Remember, not everything has to resonate with you, but if you feel a particular resistance to something as we go along, ask yourself, how come? I will do that a lot throughout the book—ask you to pause and think about what is coming up for you—so take your time and know that this journey we're on together isn't a race to a finish line; in fact, there *is* no finish line, just a path that you get to choose to carry on down every day.

Reparenting yourself while parenting your children, unlearning the patterns you might have been given and developing your own path is tough, but so are you.

Take a deep breath, and let's begin . . .

Section 1

How we got here (and why it matters)

I am a firm believer in the power of looking back so that we can gain an understanding of ourselves and what makes us tick, before we can look forward to the rest of our lives. Or perhaps a better way to phrase that is: as we move forward with our lives, we are always going to be looking back in some way or another to assess what is going on for us, especially as parents.

Through the chapters in section 1 we are going to talk about some of the experiences you might have faced growing up, self-gaslighting and what that means, how you respond to those experiences, and what patterns have emerged for you that might impact your parenting. We're going to look at what it means to grow up with a toxic parent or in a toxic dynamic, ways we can start setting boundaries and when the ultimate boundary of no contact might be right for you.

Be kind to yourself moving through this section. It is challenging to look backward sometimes, but I am here with you, and we can go as slowly as you need.

Chapter 1

Let's look back
(so we can move forward)

Parenting after growing up in a toxic environment is a challenge. There is a cruel irony in the fact that those of us who have experienced childhood trauma and are striving so passionately to be the best we can be for our children, to ensure they never experience the things we did, are often the ones least equipped to do those things. If no one had ever shown you how to read, this series of lines and squiggles that make up these words in this book would be just that—lines and squiggles without meaning. So how can you be loving, nurturing and empathic with your parenting when you've never had that modeled to you? We've all seen the "oh no, I'm turning into my mother" memes, which often put a comedic spin on popular sayings that were commonly used by older people when we were growing up, like "because I said so" or "money doesn't grow on trees." But what happens when turning into your parent is something you fear or dread?

So, we look back. We get to know ourselves and how our experiences shaped us as people; we learn what might bring up uncomfortable or upsetting things for us (often referred to as "triggers" because they can—and often do—happen so suddenly and unexpectedly) and how we can navigate those moments.

It's worth noting, while I'm talking about triggers, that nothing triggers you quite like becoming a parent and raising children. There are so many different significant moments that bring up an influx of feelings and emotions that can be overwhelming and difficult to work through. The moments when you look at your children and think, "How could you? I would never treat these beautiful little humans the way you treated me, even when parenting is the toughest." You might wonder how your parent could have hit you, shut you out for days on end, belittled you in front of other people, put alcohol or drugs in front of you, let someone else hurt you or constantly picked at your self-worth. It might be none of those things or all of them, but the point remains that those moments come thick and fast when we are raising our own children.

I remember sitting in one of my kids' first school performances and having a feeling of deep sadness and anger. I was always involved in performing at elementary school—I wasn't into sports, so my options for hobbies in the nineties were limited. I was a very overweight child, prone to eating my feelings and raised without healthy boundaries surrounding food, but immersed in diet culture and the shame that comes with it. As a result I was badly bullied for my size, which only made the cycle of overeating to feel better worse. Had I not had the stigma of being so overweight and been bullied in my younger years to early teens, not to mention been exposed to my mother's deep hatred of sports, I think I probably would have been a sporty child. I loved hockey and lacrosse, but when I had to leave the coveted private school my mother had insisted I attend to go to the local public school, due to financial disputes between my parents—all of which I was made very aware of—there was no hockey or lacrosse team, something my mother would remind me of often, as if going to the local public school was a "fall from grace."

When I was about 13 or 14 I started martial arts, which I continued for four years, gaining a black belt and an instructor certificate, but I still refer to myself as "not sporty" to this day. I was a drama kid, a singer and a musician, and that suited my mom fine. I remember one occasion at elementary school: I must have been eight or nine, and I'd been chosen to have a part in our production of *Sweeney Todd* (an unusual choice for little children to perform, but sure). I don't remember all the specifics, but I'm pretty confident I was one of the main characters, maybe even Mrs. Todd, and I had a big solo to perform. I was so nervous—I don't think I ever truly enjoyed performing the way my mom thought I did. A day or two before the performance I was told that my mom and dad were going to struggle to make it because it was on the same day as a court date for their divorce proceedings. I remember my mom telling me that "Daddy won't agree to an adjournment" and me pleading with her to rearrange, to do something so that she could be there, so both of them could be.

As an adult, I can understand the importance of finalizing divorce proceedings—after all, it was only a little school play. What creates the discomfort when I reflect on this memory is the knowledge that it was within their control, as parents, to either agree to move the date, or if that was going to make it too far away, to sit down and have a gentle, loving discussion with their child in a way that was supportive and reassuring, not filled with blame and point-scoring. It was an extremely big deal to eight- or nine-year-old Harriet, who was still clinging on to the hope that one day a *Parent Trap* situation would occur and the nightmare of my parents' vicious divorce would be over.

On the day of the play, I remember asking my teachers constantly if they could see my parents in the crowd, if they had managed to get out of court early for me. Eventually it was my turn to go on stage. It was about two-thirds of the way through the show, and as the nerves raged inside me and I walked up the side steps, I spotted not just my mom but also my dad standing on opposite sides of the grand double doors. They were smiling like they'd truly achieved something, leaning against opposite doorposts and occasionally sneering at one another. My dad had to "shoot off" at the end of the performance, but he briefly stopped to tell me how impressed he was, and I remember feeling awkward and uncomfortable with this man I'd once adored, now a stranger to me. Mom made sure to let me know that his partner had been waiting for him because she wasn't welcome at my show, and he had to be loyal to her first and leave me. I tell you all of this because, sitting there in that little school auditorium watching my own kids on stage, I felt so much sadness and anger bubble up as I wondered why it was so hard for them to just be there for me. And maybe it was the case of a scorned and angry mother and an absent, self-obsessed and avoidant father who had his priorities all wrong. It wasn't fair, and seeing how excited my kids were to have me and my husband there really triggered me.

In my own journey of healing and cycle breaking, I have discovered that alongside moments of recognition of my parents' abuse and toxic behaviors, memories of childhood experiences have resurfaced frequently. For a lot of people who experienced childhood trauma, especially those who have complex post-traumatic stress disorder, borderline personality disorder, or other mental health issues as a result, childhood memories are patchy or, in some cases, entirely absent. One of the wonderful things about our brain is that it does a mighty fine job of trying to protect us. When your experiences as a child are so toxic, even if you're not fully able to view them as such at the moment (we'll discuss this in chapter 2), the brain refuses to allow us to remember them. This goes beyond the usual memory losses that we all have— the ones that crop up around the dinner table at Christmas when a family member, friend or sibling says something about a family trip they remember from when you were seven and you have no recollection, or someone says, "Doesn't my new puppy look like Uncle Tim's old dog, the one we used to pretend was a show pony and get to jump over brooms in the garden on a leash?" and you'd totally forgotten the game, the dog and maybe even Uncle Tim! Those are part and parcel of getting older, living a full life and your brain having to pick and choose what is relevant and necessary to you in the now (I just wish mine wouldn't consider the *Monster High* soundtrack my daughter has been playing on repeat quite so relevant this week!).

Think of your brain as one big storage unit, filled with boxes and files that are stuffed full of all of your memories. The boxes nearest to the front are likely to be current things, bigger things you feel stressed or anxious about and the day to day. The further back we go in the unit, the more we find things that happened to us in childhood. The boxes are there, filled to the brim, but maybe with the odd lid that hasn't been lifted for a time. Now imagine a locked filing cabinet at the back—it can't be accessed because there are so many things in front of it, but it's jammed full. *That* is where the brain shoves the childhood memories that are simply too traumatic to deal with, and for some people, myself included, there are whole chunks of childhood memories—sometimes years and years—in that locked filing cabinet. I have very few memories between the ages of four and seven; as I've worked on healing my inner child and processed some of my trauma, a lot of memories have resurfaced, but a lot still refuse to come. The ones that do resurface often come alongside some parenting moment, whether significant or insignificant.

Throughout the chapters in this section of the book, we're going to look at what it means to grow up in a toxic family dynamic and how that affects you as a person and a parent. We will look at the different behaviors of toxic parents, many of which I'm sure you will relate to if you're reading this book, and how you can overcome the way they impact you. Finally, we will look at debt mindset and how to combat it.

Chapter 2

Growing up with a toxic family dynamic

There is nothing quite like growing up in a dysfunctional family unit with toxic parents—even reading that, you might be inclined to make excuses or feel guilty for acknowledging your parents' toxicity, depending on where you are in your healing journey. Perhaps the word "toxic" doesn't feel right for you and it seems gentler, kinder, to consider them "emotionally immature" or "incapable." That's OK, we will talk more later about acknowledging abuse or toxic behavior while also maintaining empathy and understanding.

Here's the thing that needs to be remembered when we look back at our childhood experiences on our journey toward breaking the cycle: children are blank canvases. Research into epigenetics (the study of inheritable traits, which can include behavioral patterns) and generational trauma suggests that *our very DNA can be altered by a previous generation's trauma.* We may well have a predisposition to certain traits—a "nature," if you like—but nurture informs the bulk of our development. How we connect with other humans is established in our early years through the attachments we develop with our primary caregivers—often referred to later in life as our attachment style. How we feel about ourselves, our relationships and the world at large is learned. We're born and our only behaviors are instinctual—sucking, gripping, etc. *Everything else is learned.*

Babies learn that if they cry, someone will pick them up or attend to their needs; toddlers learn that there are consequences to actions like biting or slapping, and even though they are still overwhelmed by the same frustrations and big emotions, they learn to communicate, or more often suppress, those feelings. In addition to being this wonderful blank canvas of a human who will be molded by their experiences and what they learn from those around them, a child is hardwired as a mammal to trust and seek connection with their primary caregiver, usually a mother.

Entire psychological theories are based on the importance of the relationship between parent and child—in all honesty, there aren't really any that don't at least accept that our parents or primary caregivers play a fundamental role in our development. Numerous studies into people who struggle with complex post-traumatic stress disorder as a result of being raised in traumatic homes support the theory that our brains experience physiological changes when stress is our ever-present companion and becomes our "norm."

Constantly increased levels of the stress hormone cortisol during development have been linked to numerous physiological illnesses and ailments. In fact, a study conducted by Vincent Felitti et al. in 1998, often referred to as the Adverse Childhood Experiences Study, or simply ACE, found a correlation between the leading causes of death in adults and the dysfunction and abuse in their childhoods. In layman's terms, the more adverse childhood experiences a patient has had (i.e. the higher their ACE score, which ranges between 0 and 10), the higher their risk of having health concerns associated with adverse childhood experiences.

This might seem incredibly daunting to learn, but I'm not trying to worry or scare you, just to underline how deeply trauma affects us. What's even more interesting is that those with moderate to high ACE scores are often completely unaware of their trauma, until there is a catalyst for them to look more closely at their experiences. Frequently this happens later in life when they have their own children, a parent dies or they start to work on healing issues that they had no idea were connected to their past.

When you grow up in a toxic environment, you learn a different set of behaviors and patterns. You learn to read the unspoken words, the slam of a car door, the tone of someone's footsteps in the corridor, the meaning behind how they stir their tea and how you should adjust your behavior accordingly. You learn to base your worth and sense of self on what your parent needs and expects of you, to suppress your true self and to self-abandon, to the point where many survivors of childhood trauma don't really know themselves or have a sense of self at all.

One of the most widely accepted theories surrounding childhood trauma and how continual stress affects us is Dr. Stephen Porges's polyvagal theory. Polyvagal theory proposes that the vagus nerve (part of the autonomic system—which we can think of a bit like our "internal safety hub") is responsible for creating different physiological and emotional responses in us when we communicate. We move between the stages of feeling safe (ventral vagal), mobilized (sympathetic vagal), where we feel threatened and spurred into action, and immobilized (dorsal vagal), where we become frozen, depressed or disassociated.

Children who grow up in toxic environments are often stuck navigating an almost continual cycle of mobilized to immobilized states, never reaching safety and becoming stuck in one or more of the survival responses that are referred to as the "autonomic ladder." When we are continually dysregulated as children, this becomes the norm and often transfers into adulthood. While we may learn to manage our behaviors better as adults, during times of high stress or when we are triggered by something in our past, these behaviors bubble up to the surface. It's not uncommon for these patterns of behavior to mirror our parents' survival responses too—for example, children who grow up in homes where there is a lot of shouting and arguing often slip into a fight response as adults during arguments or when they feel threatened (i.e. when their sympathetic nervous system is triggered). While this seems logical, when all of your attention as a parent is on breaking cycles to be better for your own child, to be as different from your abusive parent as possible, it can be really difficult to accept and reflect on those behaviors within yourself.

See if you recognize any of these responses within yourself, and be honest. This book is here to get to the nitty-gritty of who we are, without shame or judgment. If we want to be the best version of ourselves as parents and people, we need to know how our experiences have shaped us, and become self-aware so we can catch when habits and behaviors we don't like pop up.

Fight response

This is one of the most common survival responses, often talked about hand in hand with the flight response. When you think of an animal who is backed into a corner, they have two main ways to defend themselves—flight, where they flee as far as possible, or fight, where they make themselves as big as possible and become aggressive. For a child, flight isn't really an option—after all, where are you going to go when the person harming you is your parent, who controls your home, your financial situation and so on? So instead you learn to defend yourself. Defense is a good thing to keep in mind when you think of the fight response; while these are all responses to high stress or being triggered, fight is often the most demonized response because of the overt nature of a lot of the behaviors.

People who are stuck in a fight response are often defensive and/or aggressive when they become upset, and they might be inclined to lash out with harsh words or even physically. The likelihood is that they respond poorly to authority and perhaps struggled with behavior at school; now, as adults, they struggle with maintaining workplace relationships, especially with management. Their responses are often very explosive and unpredictable, and they're perhaps described as someone with a "short fuse." During childhood, and often into adulthood, they might have a tendency to bully others as a way of protecting themselves from any potential threats and deflecting the attention away from themselves. Adults stuck in fight mode, or who have patterns of fight-mode behaviors when triggered or overwhelmed, are prone to shouting or losing their temper quickly, but they often feel a lot of guilt in the aftermath, and even shame over the harm caused.

Flight response

"Flight" is the instinct to just *get away*, to remove yourself from the situation. This is—just like all these responses—a defensive mechanism learned over time and through modeled behavior. People who are stuck in a flight response are prone to anxiety or even panic attacks. They often have a feeling of being trapped, or they keep themselves constantly busy to avoid staying still or having to stop and process. I was very much this person when I had my first child—every day, without fail, we had some kind of baby class booked. We had baby massage, baby and toddler playgroup, music therapy, coffee with other new moms, baby yoga and at home I had a continual list of things that needed doing.

While on the surface this was commendable, in reality it was because the busier I was, the less time I had to acknowledge that being a first-time mom was bringing up a whole range of uncomfortable and triggering feelings for me, especially as I had my own mother, who was the source of a lot of my childhood traumas, living with me at the time. Micromanaging others, being emotionally unavailable and even being avoidant of relationships (or ending/sabotaging them to avoid commitment or being vulnerable) are common traits of those who struggle with the flight response, as is constantly striving to achieve or being a workaholic.

Fawn response

When we talk about "fawning" over something or someone, it often conjures the image of people surrounding a newborn baby: lots of cooing and ahhing, and everyone trying to get as close as possible so they can have their turn showing love and affection. Fawning is similar to this in the sense that, at its core, it's about *moving closer to the source of harm*, even if that means sacrificing oneself. People who are stuck in the fawn response were often emotionally or instrumentally parentified as children. Emotional parentification is when a child carries the burden of their parent's emotional needs, such as standing in as a shoulder to cry on or helping navigate relationship dramas. Instrumental parentification refers to children taking on the more physical adult responsibilities such as raising siblings or paying for household things. This leads to them becoming people-pleasers, who struggle to say no or speak up, and frequently self-abandon to fulfill the role others need of them.

Freeze response

The freeze response is often linked with depression—it can present as numbness and feelings of everything being pointless or hopeless. Ever considered yourself a "negative Nancy" or a "pessimist"? Well, that could be your freeze response. Think of a deer when it is startled by headlights—it stops, doesn't it? Everything freezes. Despite the fact that it's about to be hit by a car steamrolling toward it, everything locks up and it just stops, stuck.

The freeze response works in a similar way—it holds us back. It might manifest similarly to depression, or it could even be more simplistic, presenting as endless social media doomscrolling, procrastination, indecision or giving up quickly when faced with seemingly minor inconveniences. People who are stuck in a freeze response are prone to giving the silent treatment or shutting down communication. Just like that deer in the headlights, they are stuck and unable to find a path through the stress they are experiencing, so withdrawing into themselves and freezing out the world is the solution.

Do any of these sound familiar? Do all of them? Take some time to reflect and take a look at the task below:

Cycle breaker's toolkit: Task for self-reflection

Take a moment to look at some of the behaviors present within the fight, flight, fawn and freeze responses. Do you recognize any of these behaviors in yourself when you're especially stressed or triggered?

In your journal, write down the behaviors that you notice in yourself when you are particularly stressed, overwhelmed or triggered. Perhaps you have a tendency to "make it right" when you have a disagreement with a partner (fawn response), or maybe you find yourself shouting a lot and becoming aggressive or especially defensive (fight response).

Now take a look at the behaviors you notice show up for you—and it's important to remember not to judge yourself, but to view this as impartially as you can. Ask yourself, do different behaviors show up in different relationships? Make a note of where you notice these behaviors showing up the most.

Ask yourself where these behaviors come from—can you remember a lot of shouting and aggression during arguments growing up, and is this a habit you've picked up? Do you have a parent who was always modeling compliance or fawning toward their partner and you've become someone who just wants to keep the peace? It could be that you have gone completely the opposite way from your own parents—maybe you notice that you are avoidant and detached when your parent was angry and a bully.

Finally, consider how these responses show up in your parenting, and how it makes you feel to recognize that.

Here's an example. In my relationship with my eldest child, who has hit his teen years and is forming his own identity, I have found myself struggling not to slip into a fight response and lose my temper with him when he is pushing boundaries: shouting at him instead of communicating, and being a version of myself that frankly I don't like. I recognize a lot of the behaviors he exhibits from myself when I was younger, and it's been triggering for me. As a child I was shouted at a lot, often physically threatened and then belittled/laughed at when I showed fear or, worse in my eyes as a child with abandonment fears, ignored for days on end. While I have never done this to my own children, the watered-down version of shouting and losing my cool is still something I don't feel proud of, and it's a behavior that I would like to be able to navigate better. It is, unfortunately, a

part of that unhealthy blueprint I've been given and one of
the ways in which I have to work harder to step outside of
that fight response. We will talk later on about making
parental mistakes—which we will all make—and modeling
accountability when you do, but for now, just try to recognize
the behaviors and where they come from.

There are no right or wrong answers to these questions;
this task is here to help you practice being self-aware and
reflecting on your behaviors. We can't address or relearn
what we are unaware of.

Classic behaviors and traits of a toxic parent

The word "toxic" springs up a lot across social media, and you
might be questioning whether or not it is fair to label a person
as "toxic." After all, despite their failings, parenting is hard
and we all have room for growth and change.

While that is true, let's think about the word "toxic"—the
dictionary defines it as:

1. Poisonous.
2. Very harmful or unpleasant in a pervasive or
   insidious way.

There is very little that is more harmful or unpleasant
than a parent who neglects, mistreats or otherwise abuses
their child, and while our parents can choose to heal their
own trauma and change their behaviors, it has been my experience that the types of parents who create people who go on

to speak out about their generational trauma and become conscious cycle breakers are rarely willing to do that.

You will come across terms like "emotionally immature" or "narcissistic" when learning about toxic parents—both are valid. During an interview with psychotherapists and authors Helen Villiers and Katie McKenna on my podcast *Unfollowing Mum*, Helen, who is a specialist in narcissism and adult survivors of childhood trauma due to parental abuse, mentioned that these terms really mean the same thing—a parent who is emotionally immature will display narcissistic behaviors. I think one of the biggest areas of confusion surrounds the difference between "narcissism" (which is something we all have to a degree) and narcissistic personality disorder (NPD). Helen talks about "healthy narcissism," which is a trait that we could all display—that drive for a bigger house, a nice new car, a raise at work or even to look our best for a night out, which are all examples of healthy narcissism. This type of narcissism is non-exploitative, it's not entitled or cruel and it is a means to fulfilling needs or wants that you have without being detrimental to others. It allows you to develop your self-worth and sit within a place of high self-esteem without dragging others down. This might surprise you—after all, it's not the picture painted for us of narcissism in popular culture today, and it certainly won't sound like your toxic parent. That is where *unhealthy* narcissism, narcissistic behaviors and emotional immaturity come into play.

At its core, unhealthy narcissism will always come at the *detriment of others*, be that the narcissist putting someone down with snide remarks to make themselves feel better, pitting siblings against each other to create drama and conflict in order to swoop in and feel needed, or simply being relentlessly self-centered. When we talk about narcissistic parents, it's possible to be open and transparent about their behaviors—or narcissistic tendencies—without trying to diagnose them with a disorder. You may also have heard the terms "covert" and "overt" narcissism. We can use these terms when reflecting on toxic parental behaviors. I've often used the analogy that you don't need to be a zoologist to identify a tiger, but you might not be able to tell the type, gender or health of the tiger without some training. The same is true for a narcissistic parent—they are a tiger: the narcissistic behaviors or "orange and black stripes" are there, but these could be due to a number of reasons that don't extend to a personality disorder, and we aren't qualified to diagnose our parent with NPD in the same way we aren't able to tell too much about the genealogy of the tiger in the zoo.

When you think of a narcissist, you will more than likely think of an overt narcissist: someone who is very self-absorbed, can't be challenged in any way because they are *always* right, behaves like a toddler, lashes out when upset and always lacks empathy or avoids any accountability. They need you to admire them constantly—if it isn't about them and how great they are, it doesn't matter. This parent is cruel in an "obvious" way, usually behind closed doors, or if in public their jibes are at your expense to make themselves seem grander. Think of most toxic parental figures in popular TV shows or movies (such as Matilda's self-absorbed and grandiose parents) and you have yourself someone who exhibits overt narcissistic abuse or tendencies.

What about covert narcissism? Covert narcissism is somewhat harder to distinguish as toxic behavior. Danu

Morrigan writes in her book *You're Not Crazy, It's Your Mother: Understanding and Healing for Daughters of Narcissistic Mothers* that covert narcissism seems to be more common in mothers, whereas overt narcissism seems to be more prevalent in fathers. Jealous and envious behavior, passive aggression, centering themselves as a victim even when they've caused harm, a lack of self-awareness or empathy, and self-centeredness are all common with a covert narcissist. You might find that they have a high sensitivity to being challenged or criticized, and their public image is very different from their private image. Ringing any bells?

All of these traits, both overt and covert, are part of emotional immaturity. Think of a narcissist as a toddler who can't get their own way and hasn't yet learned to deal with it—this is a great way to help you navigate the terminology you use when identifying your parent's behaviors.

It's worth noting here that a lot of the behaviors we accept are toxic and abusive also stem from our parent's own traumas. Unhealthy narcissism and NPD in particular are widely believed to be responses to trauma, or not having one's needs met as a child. While this is true, I believe it's important to be aware that we can have compassion for the experiences that have led our parents to become the people they are, while simultaneously refusing to be complicit in their abuse of us and holding them accountable. One of my favorite phrases that I teach clients is, "We must not confuse empathy with enabling, or being compassionate with being complicit in our own abuse." You can, and must, protect your own mental health and personal space.

I could write an entire book on narcissistic parental behaviors, the terminology we use to describe our parents and why it's important for us as the survivors of abuse to name and understand the way we were treated, but that isn't our purpose here. This brief overview of narcissism, and the following descriptions of behaviors and experiences we may have had, is merely setting a foundation of understanding for what has brought you to where you are today as a cycle breaker. At the back of the book there is a comprehensive list of resources (page 283) that can help you gain a deeper understanding of not just yourself, but all the things we discuss throughout, including narcissism, parental abuse and childhood trauma. I would actively encourage you to continue learning and researching. Knowledge is power; it gives you the freedom to accept that this wasn't your fault, and your parent's or caregiver's behaviors are not within the realm of your control or responsibility, but *your* behaviors are.

So, what are some of the behaviors we might have experienced that are common within a toxic home environment and what impact do they have on us?

Childhood emotional neglect

Childhood emotional neglect is a term that's being discussed more frequently; alongside other types of emotional abuse, it's beginning to receive the gravitas that it deserves in order for us to work through it and heal as adults. When you think of neglect, your mind will more than likely jump straight to a child who is left for hours or days on end, perhaps in dirty diapers or without food, unable to care for themselves and without anyone to care for their basic needs. While many of us may have experienced this type of abuse, and the impact it has on us as adults is huge, there are many who may have had their basic physical needs met, but their emotional needs were neglected with the same level of callousness and indifference. The sticking point for emotional neglect, for any type of emotional abuse, is often how society, and by proxy how we, perceive it to be "less" damaging, when research suggests that isn't the case at all.

Consider for a moment Maslow's Hierarchy of Needs (see below). Maslow's theory emerged in 1943, initially as a study into human motivation, but over time it has become one of psychology's underpinning theories and is widely accepted as a basis for understanding how we develop and what our needs are. Today we understand Maslow's theory as stating that we have a pyramid of needs, each one built upon a foundation of physiological needs such as breathing, food, physical touch and water. If we don't have those most basic needs met, we

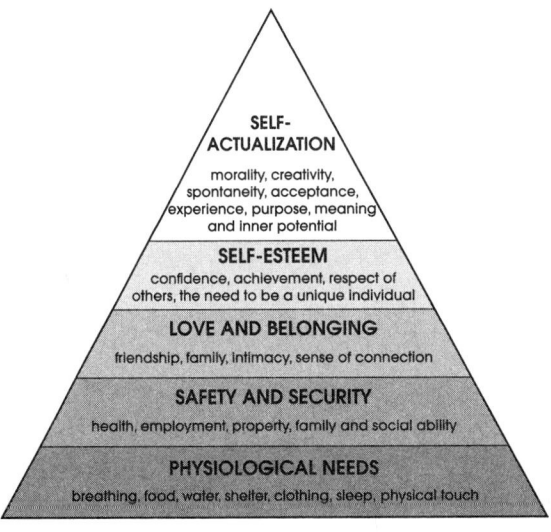

can't progress to the next stage of the pyramid and meet other needs. Seems simple enough, right?

We put such emphasis and importance on the "basic needs" in society, and yet according to Maslow's theory, over half of those needs are emotional. It begs the question: why do we dismiss the impact of emotional abuse such as childhood emotional neglect? Often what we find with emotional neglect is that one or more of the stages on the pyramid have been ignored or skipped—perhaps we had safety, a "roof over our head" and parents who didn't fit into any of the classic abuser categories, but we didn't have love or belonging. We might look back and see that we sought to fulfill these needs by striving harder for esteem, be that at school, through high grades or sports achievements, or perhaps within a friendship group, where we acted in ways that didn't align with who we were; or perhaps we became stuck, unable to move past that lack of love and belonging and acting out in anger from a core belief that we were never enough. When one of these needs is missing, the others can't compensate.

In her book *Adult Children of Emotionally Immature Parents*, Lindsay Gibson notes that adult children of emotionally immature parents who have experienced emotional neglect often follow one of two paths: they become internalizers or they become externalizers. Internalizers do exactly what the name implies—they internalize their negative experiences with their toxic parents. They are often very reflective and passionate about learning and healing, but they run the risk of becoming people-pleasers and taking on too much of the emotional labor in relationships, becoming resentful in the process. Internalizers are attached to the idea that *they* hold the power to change their circumstances and meet their own needs, but sometimes also that they hold the power to change others too. They would have been the child who tried their hardest to please their parents with good grades, sporting achievements and constant approval-seeking to feel like they were "enough." They may well have gone on to become high-achieving adults, but they always feel there is something missing, or have a sense of never feeling fulfilled or reaching self-actualization at the top of the pyramid.

By contrast, externalizers hold firm to the belief that someone else needs to come along and fix their problems or fulfill their needs, and nothing they do will ever account for the "lack" in their life. They are often impulsive or reactive, sometimes displaying their own narcissistic tendencies and feeling entitled or owed by the world. Externalizers would be the children who became stuck, unable to move forward into adulthood and become responsible for fulfilling their own needs or break out of the cycle of anger and hurt they are in. As children they often mimic the toxic parent, in the subconscious hope that the parent will "see" them and meet the needs they are neglecting.

At this point you might be able to see how the patterns of generational trauma emerge. Perhaps you have siblings who mirror your toxic parent, or you recognize that, in your younger years, you did. Because you're reading this book, you've probably reached a point where you've become aware that your patterns of behavior are no longer serving you, especially in healing your childhood trauma. Or maybe you've moved past this point and addressed some of these internalizing or externalizing behaviors, but you fear the cycle repeating with your own children. Whether you internalize or externalize, it can be detrimental to your healing, and finding a balance is key. We will look a bit more at finding balance between internalizing and externalizing in chapter 9. For now, you will find some helpful journaling prompts at the end of this section. Here you can consider what area of your emotional needs was neglected, and self-reflect on how you have responded to that as you've grown into adulthood. As always, be kind and gentle with yourself, and remember you are not responsible for the choices or behavior of your parent.

Parentification

Parentification takes various forms, but it is, much like emotional neglect, something that is rarely discussed when it is solely emotional. Parentification happens when we place our children in a role that is better suited to an adult caregiver or the parent themselves, often in exchange for the parent taking on the role of the child. As we discussed briefly in chapter 2, there are two types of parentification—instrumental and emotional. Let's take a deeper look.

Instrumental parentification requires the child to take on practical roles within the home—caring for younger siblings or a sick parent, doing chores and/or other physical activities—that are unsuitable for their age. Emotional parentification requires the child to take on emotional roles within the home, perhaps becoming a mediator for warring parents, a sounding board or "best friend" for a parent or even stepping into the role of spouse, sometimes leading to emotional or "covert" incest. As mentioned above, emotional parentification is often the forgotten side of the abusive behavior coin, as the acts can be so subtle and easily missed. The damaging effects of parentification are huge, and yet there is a lot of excusing or gaslighting when it comes to the topic. Adult children who discuss the experience will often hear things like, "Well, she just needed someone to talk to, she was lonely," or, "But they were ill/a single parent, so you had to help them with the younger children! What did you expect them to do?" However, while those things might be explanations for *why* parentification occurs, they aren't excuses.

I was heavily emotionally parentified as a child. It felt like I became my mother's stand-in spouse and sounding board from the age of four. On my podcast, *Unfollowing Mum*, I've spoken with guests who have shared that their parent would expect them to listen to inappropriate and detailed discussions of sexual exploits at a young age (this is also an example of covert sexual abuse). In my case, by the age of 12 or 13 this was such a deeply ingrained part of our relationship that I was responsible for choosing kitchen layouts and paint colors, then criticized when I grew older and said they no longer matched my tastes. I grew up feeling responsible for my mother's happiness, always suppressing myself and my needs to cater to hers, and it has taken me years of self-work to get to a point where I am comfortable and able to set firm boundaries. People who experience parentification often become people-pleasers and struggle with codependency, a lack of boundaries and no sense of self. It can take years of healing work, some of the most effective of which is believed to be inner child work. At the end of this section of the book, you will find some inner child guided journal prompts, and if you recognize these feelings in yourself, I would urge you to give them a try.

Triangulation

This is a common tool in the toxic parent toolbox and one that many people experience, though it might be especially familiar to you if you have siblings. Triangulation is simply a method of manipulation whereby a third party is brought into a dispute, or a "triangle" is created to isolate and control parties within the family. We often hear triangulation referred to as "playing off against one another" or "divide and conquer" because that is the intention, especially when a parent seeks to triangulate siblings or the other parent.

A very common example growing up might have been if you had a toxic parent who loved to compare you to your sibling, but always in a negative light and usually in a manner that created a divide and allowed little to no communication between you. They might have said things like, "Oh, you got a B in science? Your brother's favorite subject has always been science, he used to get A+ all the time," without acknowledging you or your achievement. Perhaps you both experienced this behavior, or perhaps either you or your sibling was always positioned as a "favorite" (often referred to in therapeutic settings as a golden child), while the other was the butt of the joke, the root of all complaints or the "black sheep" (often referred to in therapeutic settings as a scapegoat).

It's possible that this behavior extended beyond siblings, or maybe you were an only child but you noticed a lot of triangulation in which you became the go-between for your warring parents, a middleman for emotional immaturity whereby you were expected to "pass on" information or pick sides. In this scenario, one or both parents attempt to gain the support of the child, and effectively create a rift in the relationship with the other parent. This can be such a difficult and traumatizing situation—it is a type of parentification, and likewise creates people-pleasing tendencies, often forcing children to become self-disregarding and step into the role of "rescuer" in other relationships as they grow into adulthood.

There are lots of different examples of triangulation within toxic family dynamics. All of them are destructive in some way or another, often carrying on well into adulthood, especially if we start to set boundaries or our toxic parents view us as "pulling away" from their control. My personal experience with triangulation has been consistent throughout the majority of my life, until I cut ties with my mother, and even then, the attempts continued. One example I remember as an adult happened when my mother tried to create a rift between my mother-in-law and myself. At the time, I had an enmeshed relationship with my mom, despite having been married for a number of years and having my own small children. If she said something, I would assume it was correct or truthful, as had been the status quo all of my life.

Enmeshment is when you become overly connected to a person, often sacrificing your own needs, wants and desires, being utterly without boundaries and having no sense of self without that person. Enmeshed families tend to think with a hive mind, often dominated by the behavior of one parent or figurehead; the family members are unable to step outside of the core "unit." Adult children who are enmeshed with a parent are more likely to form codependent relationships, where they give their all and base their worth on the relationship and their partner's validation, and create an unhealthy dependency. Enmeshment is a common response to covert narcissistic abuse, but it is frequently dismissed in favor of describing the family unit as "just really close."

In an example of triangulation, my mom came to me deeply upset over a message she claimed was sent to her work email from my mother-in-law, demanding that she remove her from her contacts. Mom felt it was rude and abrupt, without provocation. I was appalled and deeply defensive of my mom—how dare my mother-in-law upset her so? I spoke to my husband, Adam, and we both agreed that this needed addressing, much to my mom's surprise. Normally there would have been anger, a bit of "freezing out" of the party who had upset us, but never direct conversation. I remember her telling us not to bother about it, it wasn't that big of a deal, but Adam was firm: he was going to speak to his mother and get to the bottom of it. I'm sure you can guess where this is going? There was no evidence of any emails. When challenged later on, my mom became angry and insisted she had deleted them and that she just wasn't good with technology, and that my mother-in-law had probably planned this all along. I'm assuming her intention here was to create a rift between myself and my mother-in-law in order to center herself and continue to be the primary female figure in my life. *But triangulation doesn't work when it's combatted with open, honest communication.* Adam's relationship with his own parent had a foundation in mutual respect and boundaries, and that allowed him the space to challenge his mother and question her, which is something that, at the time, I had never felt empowered to do with my own.

When it comes to toxic grandparents, one of their most powerful tools is triangulation. As a cycle breaker, if you are still in contact with or you choose to allow your children to have contact with your parent, and you recognize this behavior from your childhood, be mindful and aware of the signs. Teaching your children to set boundaries from a young age is incredibly powerful, and something that the majority of us have had to learn on our own. Simple phrases like "Please don't talk about Mommy/Daddy like that around me, it upsets me" hold a lot of power in challenging triangulation, but the most powerful tool of all is open communication. We dive into boundaries briefly in chapter 4, and look further into helping your child to set them in section 3 of the book, as well as some useful scripts you may wish to teach them.

I believe my eldest child experienced a lot of triangulation from my mom, as she was very much a part of our lives for the first decade of his, including living with us. There have been so many things that he has only felt empowered to tell us about *after* we cut contact with her, yet in addition to the sadness we've felt in discovering the way she treated him, I do feel proud of the boundaries he told us he would often set with her. She would be negative about me, his dad and, for reasons only known to her, his little brother when we weren't around, allow him to miss school if we had trusted her to look after the kids, buy him gifts and tell him that his younger siblings were the "favorites" of his parents, but he was hers. She would repeat behaviors from my childhood that I had suppressed or dismissed as "normal."

Our son would often say, "Don't say that about my mommy/ daddy, Maw Maw, it's not kind." And she would apologize or occasionally become defensive and say, "I'm only saying what's true!" and go back to whatever she had been doing. Being aware and creating that safe space for your child to communicate with you makes triangulation so much more challenging, and if these behaviors do show up, it is our responsibility to protect our children and set our own boundaries, and to follow through with consequences if the behavior continues.

Gaslighting

Gaslighting is a form of emotional abuse that makes you question your own reality, thoughts and feelings. It can show up in different ways, from outright lying to subtle coercion, but it is one of the most fundamental tools in a toxic family dynamic to control, undermine and ultimately emotionally assassinate someone's sense of self, especially in children.

You might remember your parent playing the victim to elicit sympathy, outright lying about events or twisting the truth to suit their agenda. Perhaps they had a public persona that stood in sharp contrast to their private self that you experienced behind closed doors, but any attempts to address this would be met with denial and dismissal from others. Experiencing gaslighting growing up has a tremendous impact on our self-esteem and confidence, especially in terms of trusting ourselves and our abilities. You're taught to gaslight yourself, always believing that you must be the problem and remaining unsure of how to set boundaries, which often leads to you having relationships in adulthood with people who exhibit similar behaviors to your parents. When our self-esteem and ability to trust our gut are so fundamentally impacted, we fall back on the instinct to look for the familiar in our relationships, and familiar to someone who grew up in a toxic dynamic *is* toxic. This becomes a vicious cycle of developing relationships with toxic people: when that all falls apart or we start questioning the red flags, it reinforces our core belief that *we* are the problem.

Adult children of toxic parents often tell me of occasions where they tried to speak to their parent about their behavior, or the behavior they experienced in childhood, only to be met with complete denial that the events ever occurred. "You're remembering it wrong," "I never said that" and "So you're saying I'm the worst mother in the world then?" are common phrases that crop up time and again, which, as noted by Danu Morrigan in her brilliant book *You're Not Crazy, It's Your Mother*, feels like a double whammy—not only do you experience the abuse in the first place, but then it's denied with such ferocity that you begin to question yourself.

One of the things I've found really helpful in reclaiming power from gaslighting is to step outside of the emotional situation and view it with objectivity. Remember the acronym DARVO, which shows how toxic people follow a classic pattern in gaslighting:

- Deny/defend
- Attack
- Reverse
- Victim (role)
- Offender (role)

Let's look at DARVO in action.

Think of a scenario in which you have confronted your parent—it might be when they have made toxic comments about your weight or a new job, been rude to a partner or overstepped boundaries with your kids. Now break the conversation down as follows:

Behavior Pattern	Might look like . . .
Deny/Defend	"Oh, I didn't say that, you must have misheard me." "I didn't mean it like that." "Look, I'm not perfect . . ." "I'm only human."
Attack	"Honestly, one little comment and you blow it out of proportion and ruin the day for everyone." "You always do this, you're so dramatic and sensitive." "You spoil everything with your attitude." "You're so ungrateful." "After all I've done for you . . ."
Reverse	"This is just typical because . . ." "I can't believe . . ." "I'm shocked . . ."
Victim (role)	"I guess I'm the worst parent in the world, huh?" "I am so devastated that you've said this." "I'm crushed you think this of me." "Why do you always look for the worst in people?" "You really hate me, don't you?" "All I wanted was to spend time with you/make you happy . . ."
Offender (role)	"I can't believe *you* would hurt me like this." "You've deliberately brought this up when you know I'm dealing with . . ." "You are the one with the problem . . ." "You need to go to therapy, there is something wrong with you . . ."

It's quite interesting to see how often this pattern plays out in interactions with toxic parents, but you're not alone. Being mindful of this can be so powerful in setting boundaries and stopping the behavior.

As a cycle breaker, you can teach your children about gaslighting and help them protect themselves right from the get-go, in an age-appropriate manner. One of the most powerful things we can teach our kids is that they have the ability to challenge what adults say, and have their own thoughts and feelings. They are not defined by what an adult says about them, and empowering them to trust themselves is huge.

Self-gaslighting: "Was it that bad?"

One of the most powerful things gaslighting in childhood does to us is teach us how to gaslight ourselves.

We can very quickly fall into the trap of thinking we are just dramatic, self-centered, lazy or a whole bunch of other things our negative inner critic (we'll chat about them later in the book) wants us to think when we reflect on our childhood experience.

I've lost count of every time I've thought, "Well, was it that bad?" or, "Hmm, maybe I'm making this sound worse than it was . . ." It's only reminding myself that every single client I have worked with has said the same thing, and all of my research into toxic parenting, that help me step outside of that gaslighting frame of mind.

I learned this exercise from Helen Villiers and Katie McKenna in their book *You're Not the Problem,* and it remains one of the most powerful I've used to date. If you find yourself struggling with the question "Was it really that bad?", try this:

Imagine you've been asked to write a description of a parent. On one side of a piece of paper, write about **your parent**. How did they make you feel? What kind of things did they do with you, if any? How did they speak to you, care for you? How about when you were ill? What was a typical day like with them, from morning to bedtime? You can include as much detail as you feel able to.

Now write about your **ideal parent**. How would you feel around them? What would an average day be like? What would you do together? How would they care for you, speak to you? Think about their body language, tone and facial expressions. Be realistic but honest. It's not unrealistic to expect to be treated with love and compassion.

Note the difference between your two descriptions. It's OK to acknowledge it was that bad.

Covert sexual abuse/emotional incest

When we think of sexual abuse we often think, understand-ably, of overt sexual abuse. The term "incest" might bring up a range of feelings for you, but emotional incest/covert sexual abuse is much more common than you might think.

Sexual abuse is sadly not an uncommon experience for many children. According to a study conducted by the NSPCC, around 1 in 20 children aged between 11 and 17 will face sexual abuse. Despite this horrifying stat, we rarely hear about covert sexual abuse—in fact, many of us have never heard the term at all. I want to focus on covert sexual abuse as it's something that I find an alarming number of people with toxic parents, myself included, have experienced in some form, and there is an intense shame and dismissal of it.

I want to clarify that not including a section on overt sexual abuse does not minimize or dismiss the trauma of that experience. But if you talk about covert sexual abuse, it's often shrugged off, or worse, seen as an insult to "real" victims of sexual abuse. However, much as physical and emotional abuse shouldn't be compared and placed in some kind of bizarre competition, neither should covert and overt sexual abuse. Covert sexual abuse is an insidious and deeply traumatic experience that leads to internal shame, a lack of self-worth and the potential for later mental health struggles.

Covert sexual abuse can take many forms, from discussing sexual exploits in detail with a child, to insisting on bathing or changing them way past the age at which it is necessary to do so, to engaging in sexual activity when there is a child in the room or when a parent is aware a child can hear/see, or encouraging an excessive interest in sex and sexual exploration. On the podcast, we've discussed stories of parents having phone or physical sex when their child was next to them, bathing a child who was almost adolescent and physically able to bathe themselves, and a parent discussing sexual experiences in detail from a very young age. From my own experience as a young adult, my mother gave me an internal examination while 40 weeks pregnant to see if the baby was engaged, because she claimed to have trained as a midwife before I was born (there are questions around this, and while she worked in nursing, she was not a registered midwife).

Jennette McCurdy touched on covert sexual abuse in her book *I'm Glad My Mom Died*, though she didn't label it as such. It created deep discussion on social media about what covert sexual abuse actually looks like. I believe I was raised as a stand-in spouse, similar to the examples of parentification we've seen; I was relied upon to fulfill those needs, but with a disregard of my own needs as a child. So normalized are these covert behaviors in society that we often see them present in the "toxic boy mom" culture, where the mother can't let go of her son, or declares him her "first love," or sobs on his wedding day because his new partner is "taking him away." This goes beyond the standard sadness we feel when our children grow up and develop their own lives, leaving us with an "empty nest," and places a projection of our need for intimacy and partnership onto the child.

Abuse of any kind is about control, and covert sexual abuse is no different. Toxic parents often feel a sense of entitlement to their child on such a deeply rooted level that they feel a degree of ownership of their body, mind and soul. I remember my mom telling me on many occasions, "That's not your belly button, it's mine! I made it!", and while this might have been a harmless joke, it sends the message to a child that their body is not their own and sets a dangerous precedent for empowering them to be secure in their bodily autonomy. Being mindful to teach our children that they are the keepers of *their* bodies is hugely important, from explaining basic tasks to them, like, "Hey, I'm going to wash your legs here because you've got dirty and need some help cleaning up, OK?", to encouraging them to take on those tasks themselves as they get older. Even things as simple as knocking on doors to let them know you're entering can be really empowering.

When it comes to sex, we want to empower the next generation and remove the stigma and shame associated with it, especially for girls. The rule of thumb I follow is to allow *them* to ask you any questions and answer them as openly and honestly as possible in an age-appropriate manner. I will never forget my then nine-year-old son asking me what "gang-bang" meant because he'd overheard a group of 15- and 16-year-old boys whose soccer practice started after his. Initially I was a bit taken aback—who wouldn't be? But the options were: dismiss his question, tell him this wasn't something he could know and make him feel a level of shame for asking, or explain it in an age-appropriate way. If we dismiss or shame children for curiosity, we make the topic itself shameful and disempower them. So I opted to give a factual definition that applied to the context in which he heard it. We talk a lot about consent in our house, so it's something he was already familiar with and a conversation we can start having with our children right from day one. He looked at me with a wrinkled nose and said, "Oh." That was that. By meeting his curiosity with facts, without making a fuss or creating shame around it, he was less likely to seek out the information from porn or peers, which could be damaging. Often for those of us who have experienced sexual abuse, regardless of whether it was covert or not, that shame becomes generational. In our desire to protect our children from the harm that we experienced, we stigmatize sex because of our own shame.

If these experiences resonate with you, I want to remind you that this wasn't your fault and you can let go of the shame, if you feel it. Your parent's behavior is outside the realm of your control as a child, and covert sexual abuse, by its very nature, deeply impacts us. Working with a trauma professional can be really useful for releasing shame and anger surrounding covert sexual abuse. Internal Family Systems (IFS) therapy is a particularly powerful tool in working with shame and helping to unpick it. IFS works on the principle that we all have different "parts" of ourselves that play different roles to make us who we are, all led by a true "self." We'll explore this a little later in chapters 16 and 17.

Religious or spiritual abuse

This is the weaponization of spiritual or religious beliefs in order to control or shame a child. It can look and feel different for everyone, but anything that uses religion or spirituality to control, coerce, distort your sense of self, or affect your *own* spiritual or religious beliefs is abuse. Commonly in childhood this will look like threats that if you or your loved ones don't comply or behave in a manner the abuser sees fit, you will face a consequence related to the religious belief. It might look like telling you you're not a "good" example of that particular religion, or even belittling your beliefs if you have chosen a different path than your parent, which is common with teens, who often start to discover their own sense of spirituality.

Allowing your child to feel your love through whatever religious or spiritual beliefs you have can be a beautiful and empowering thing for both of you, but as with all things in parenting, it is our job to hold space for our children to forge their own path, to feel free to discover and question, while knowing that we have a safe space for them to fall back on.

Silent treatment or stonewalling

Silent treatment has been somewhat normalized in our society, yet it is one of the most damaging and harmful behaviors in a relationship, and it is absolutely a form of emotional abuse. Growing up with a parent who practices silent treatment is a baffling experience, and one that can trigger our "fawn response" (see page 27). "Stonewalling" is another term for silent treatment, coined by psychologist and marriage expert John Gottman, because it is like hitting a stone wall of communication—no matter how hard you try, you're not getting through, and you're damaging yourself in the process of trying. Adult children of parents who routinely subjected them to bouts of silent treatment report a discomfort with silence, and hypervigilance to the world and people around them; they often describe knowing someone's mood just by the way they put the key in the door or the sound of their footsteps.

When we're children, we don't have the rationale to look at our parent's behavior as something that is their responsibility, so *we internalize everything*. We believe we have caused the problem, even on a subconscious level, and like all things that cause us hurt, we attempt to avoid this feeling of insecurity, confusion and fear by taking on the role of "fixer." This is something that you can't really do much about as a child—it creates a level of primal fear that you are being abandoned, and your very being will push against that notion—but as adults who have experienced a parent who regularly uses silent treatment to manipulate and control, we do have the power to change the situation. When someone is offering you silent treatment, the best course of action is to let them—the more you try to pander to their behavior, fix a problem that you may or may not be totally in the dark about, or demand answers, the more that person will take pleasure in your discomfort. People use silent treatment because it's an effective means to gain the attention that they believe will soothe whatever wound they feel you have caused. Open, honest communication is the solution, but the risk for them is that this might not resolve in you admitting all fault and they may be asked to do some self-reflecting— which, let's be frank, isn't on their to-do list. You can say something like, "I'm not going to beg you to talk to me, but know that I'm here when you are ready to let me know what has upset you and I will listen."

I just want to touch on the differences between someone asking for space, going no contact and "silent treatment." I've had clients in the past who have experienced prolonged and continual silent treatment from their parents from a young age and it deeply impacted their ability to set boundaries and their sense of self-worth. They were in a constant state of fawning. Their view was that if they cut contact with this parent, who would regularly refuse to speak to them for months on end without any explanation, then that would make them just as bad. The difference between asking for space, or being low or no contact with a parent, is the intention. When you have an argument with someone, you might say, "I'm going for a walk, I need some space and time to think." You might say to your own child, "I'm really angry in this moment and I need to take a few minutes in the kitchen to sit with this feeling, so please give Mommy/Daddy a minute," and take yourself off to do some breathing exercises or scream into a pillow.

You are communicating that you will be back—this is safe, this is me needing something in the moment, *but I'm coming back*. This is how healthy, mature dynamics work during disputes. With low contact it's similar, and with no contact it's a means to protect yourself—you aren't hoping for that parent to chase you, to "fix" something you haven't communicated, because you've likely been communicating your hurt for most of your life in one way or another. Your goals in any of these scenarios aren't to create panic or hurt, to make someone chase you or to manipulate a scenario to your benefit—which *are* the goals of silent treatment.

This brings me neatly to the subject of the next chapter. But before we move on from looking back at some of the behaviors you may or may not have experienced as a child, I want to remind you that it's OK if you related to a lot of this chapter, or very little. Perhaps you're now thinking, "Well, my parents have a few behaviors I don't like, but I don't think they were *bad* parents. I just want to be . . . better." We don't have to have experienced childhood trauma or childhood abuse to want to parent differently than our parents; however, many people who identify that they have cycles to break have experienced these things and may or may not be aware of how much trauma they carry or how their experiences have shaped who they are. It's OK if your relationship with your parent is now in a positive place, but you recognize that there were certain generational behaviors that were commonplace then that caused you harm, so now you are mindful of choosing a different path for your own family. It's OK to love your parents dearly, or not at all, and challenge the way they parented you. It's possible to feel let down by their parenting and have a positive relationship now with parents who are capable of self-reflection and of acknowledging the mistakes that they made. These two truths can stand side by side, and absolutely no one can tell you how your relationships should look, or how you should feel about your experience of childhood.

Cycle breaker's toolkit: Empty chair exercise

There are several ways to do this exercise; however, all of them will require you to find a place where you feel safe and where you can do the exercise without interruption and in privacy. You may wish to carry this out with a trained professional, though that isn't always essential for empty chair exercises. A good rule of thumb is to **stop if you find yourself becoming overwhelmed with emotions or distressed.**

You may wish to use a physical empty chair—be it a spot on the sofa, a kitchen chair or a bench—or you may wish to simply close your eyes and imagine a chair.

What I want you to do before you get started is a technique called "box breathing." It's really simple and something I teach to all of my clients (and my kids, because it's easy to remember and effective in calming and soothing the stressful moments in life). All you need to do is take a deep breath in for a count of four, hold for four and then breathe out for four. Repeat this four to five times. You can use box breathing any time—especially if you're feeling particularly anxious. During those times it can help to imagine you're drawing a line around a box shape and every time you get to a four count, you hit the corner of your imaginary box and change direction. For the purpose of this exercise, though, let's just focus on that breathing and, as you do, become aware of the feeling of your feet on the floor. What does it feel like? Are you wearing socks? What does the fabric feel like? Or are you barefoot? How does that feel under your toes?

This type of breathing and mindfulness of your feet is often referred to as grounding. It allows you to calm your body and feel centered in the space that you are in. Studies show that breathing out for longer than you breathe in has a calming effect on the nervous system, but we will look more into breathing exercises later in the book.

Now that you have grounded yourself, I want you to imagine that your parent (try this one at a time if you feel you have something to say to both parents) is sitting in the empty chair that is either in your mind or in front of you in the physical realm. If you find it too difficult to imagine the person, that's OK, you don't have to. The crucial part of this exercise is saying whatever it is that you need to say—no matter how embarrassing, emotional or vulnerable it is. You may wish to shout, cry or vent—there is no wrong way to express your emotions toward the person in your empty chair; however, a gentle reminder that if you feel yourself becoming overwhelmed, take a step back, remember the breathing exercise above and allow yourself to focus on the feeling of your feet on the floor.

The purpose of this exercise is to help you to identify feelings toward your parents that you may or may not be aware of and to allow you to express yourself freely, which is especially powerful if you have always been silenced or dismissed. As you are speaking to the person in your empty chair, label your feelings. You can refer to the feelings wheel, which was developed by Dr. Gloria Willcox, on the following page. The feelings wheel is a great tool, both for yourself and to share with your children as a cycle-breaking parent. We often limit ourselves to emotions that we hear about daily—anger, sadness, happiness—but actually there is a *huge* range of feelings that fall into some of those "bigger" categories, and getting yourself to recognize what you are actually feeling can be really powerful in helping you grow and get more in touch with your inner you. We often have preconceived notions or biases about what feelings are "good" or that we should allow ourselves to feel—but no feeling is inherently bad. Feelings can often act as a prompt to our brain that something needs to change or that we aren't caring for ourselves properly. Being in touch with those feelings allows us to make the changes we need or to seek help where applicable.

**EMOTION &
FEELING WHEEL**

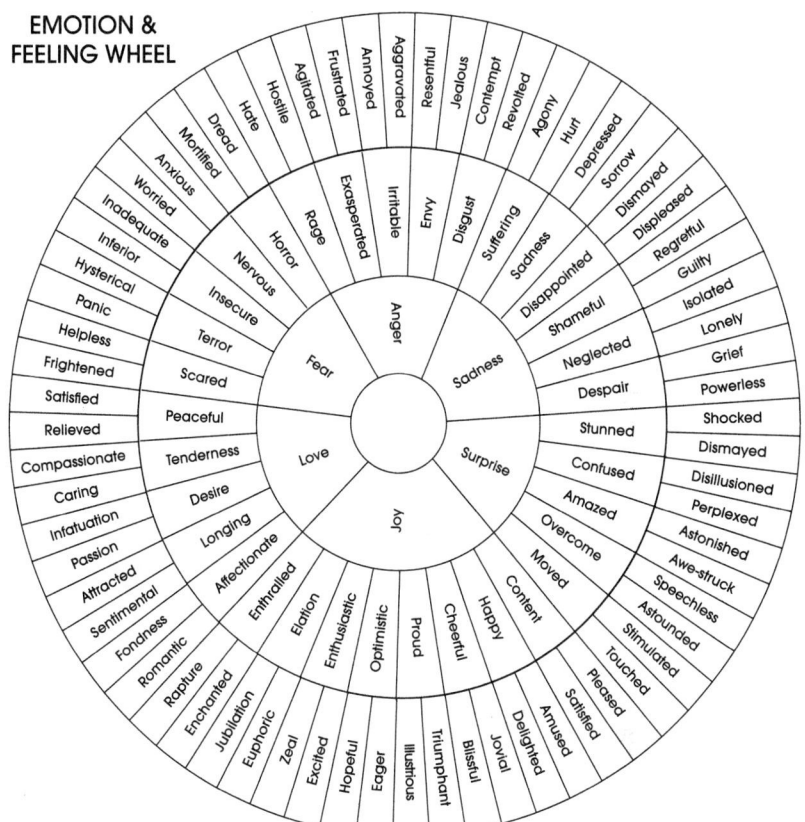

Chapter 3

Misconceptions around going low/no contact or setting boundaries with a toxic parent

I briefly touched in the last section on the difference between "silent treatment" and "no contact." This is just one of the many misconceptions surrounding estrangement, or setting boundaries with toxic parents who refuse to work on themselves and adjust their behavior.

Low or no contact: What is the difference and how do you know which is right for you?

Low-contact and no-contact relationships are both valid choices within a relationship with your parent. However, both come with their own complications, and truthfully, no one knows what is the best choice for you apart from *you*.

No contact is fairly simplistic in its method—it is exactly what the name implies: there is *no* contact. While it can come with a deep grief and healing process of its own, no contact is often a seemingly less complicated option for many. Each familial situation is unique, however, and no contact can be very complicated for some if there is childcare, a family business or other things involved. From an emotional point of view, many clients and estranged people I have spoken to over the years describe finally making the choice to be entirely no contact as a huge weight off their shoulders. Interestingly, many people also find that once they cut contact with a toxic parent, there is a deep period of processing trauma and healing that they never expected. The body holds trauma; several researchers over the years have determined that trauma has both genetic and physical links that can present as physical ailments. I'm not going to go into too much detail here, but a great place to learn more about this is *The Body Keeps the Score* by Bessel van der Kolk. What I do want to focus on is that when we were raised in toxic environments in which we continually faced new traumas, finding ourselves free from that has a huge impact.

If you find yourself feeling exhausted, finding new memories of your childhood experiences being unleashed, and feeling a deep grief for not only the loss of a relationship you should have had but for your childhood too, *that's OK.* You are far from alone, and this period of grief after estrangement is normal. Many people, especially those who experience chronic illness or stress/anxiety-related somatic symptoms, such as stomach cramps, migraines and random aches around the body, also report a sudden lift in their symptoms once they have cut contact with their abusive parent. It is as if the body breathes a deep sigh of relief, unclenching and relaxing into its new, safer life.

Be mindful that you may need additional support during this time, and that it is OK to reach out to a professional or friends if you're struggling—this doesn't have to have an impact on your choice to cut contact, or mean you must have made a mistake. If you're considering no contact, I'd invite you to think about what support you have in place to help you through this period. You might also feel ambivalent about the decision to cut contact, which is absolutely OK too.

Finally, you may feel that the decision to cut contact is outside of your control and that your parent has made the decision for you, either by telling you that they no longer want contact themselves or by not accepting the boundaries you have tried to put in place and leaving you with no choice. This can be extremely painful and difficult to make your peace with; however, the exercises throughout this book and the resources in the final section will support you and help you connect with yourself in a healing way.

Low-contact relationships are a lot more common than no-contact relationships within toxic family dynamics; in fact, it's not uncommon for us to not even really acknowledge that we have a low-contact relationship. Many people will refer to their low-contact situation by saying, "Ah, we don't really get along, so I just see them every so often," or create a physical distance between themselves and their family to avoid contact without explicitly saying that this is what they are doing (or even being aware themselves that that is what they are doing). How many of you reading this moved out of your hometown and far away as soon as you could? Perhaps you emigrated, or maybe you live nearby out of a feeling of comfort, but you avoid seeing your family as much as possible. Perhaps they avoid seeing you, and their behavior has been dismissive or ambivalent since you became an adult (or maybe even earlier). There is no hard and fast rule for what constitutes low contact—for some reading this who have experienced an enmeshed or codependent relationship, the idea of not seeing a parent once a week at least is "low contact," and for others, seeing your parent only on special occasions or less is "low contact." As with all things in our relationships, this links to our personal boundaries (which we will discuss in chapter 4) and personal comfort zone—how often you want to see your parent, if at all, is entirely up to you *and* within the realm of your control.

Low-contact relationships often tend to be met, though not always, with passive aggression as opposed to outright challenges from parents. We often slide slowly into them, tiptoeing gently away from the relationship. While they are no less valid than no-contact relationships, they are often a result of avoidance on the part of both the adult child and the parent. Direct challenges to the current situation would result in less contact, potentially none at all, and while there may be friction and discomfort, it seems less daunting to keep a distance than to address your toxic parent's behaviors and ask for change and validation.

There are a million and one reasons why someone may consciously (or subconsciously) choose to be low contact with a parent. These may include not wanting to lose the relationship with a parent you do feel you have a positive relationship with, a sense of guilt surrounding breaking contact, ill health, financial constraints, childcare, feeling the pull to facilitate a relationship between your child and their grandparent, or even a sense that it's "easier." Whatever your reason for maintaining contact with a parent, I'd invite you to consider who the contact is for, and what impact it has on you. Do you find yourself feeling sick if you see your parent's name flash up on your phone? Do you find yourself struggling to enjoy your time if you are around them? Maybe you find yourself filled with a sense of dread at the thought of a Zoom call or visit? If the answer to these questions is yes, I'd invite you to consider if you would maintain this contact in any other relationship, and if not, what keeps you maintaining it here? Are there boundaries you could put in place that would alleviate these feelings?

I'd like to just pause here. It's really important that you know there are no right or wrong answers to these questions about how you feel regarding your current situation with your parent. There is no one-size-fits-all route to take in navigating dysfunctional relationships, and in some instances you might find yourself fluctuating between no and low contact as you progress along your healing journey. You might find that having your own children cements your decision and empowers you to set firmer boundaries or sever ties altogether. *You* are in control of your relationships and the choice of who you have in your life.

Attitudes toward estrangement and low-contact relationships

Attitudes toward parents and the ways in which we should behave toward them change from culture to culture, but there are very few cultures, if any, where an adult child's right to autonomy when it comes to ending a relationship with a toxic parent is respected. In the UK where I live we have a relatively individualistic culture; it's normalized for children to grow up, head to university or move out of the family home and then begin their own lives with their own family, but still to have a level of deference to their parents. We have a culture of "stiff upper lip" here, where abuse isn't discussed and phrases like "don't air your dirty laundry" tell us that we shouldn't discuss family or personal matters in public. This makes the topic of estrangement or family dysfunction so taboo that I have lost count of the number of people I have spoken to—both as a coach and within my community online—who are utterly shocked to learn that their experiences aren't unique to them and are, in fact, quite common.

This cultural norm of moving away from home and having our own "separate" lives means that low-contact relationships, while they may still be judged by strangers, the media and other family members, are much more common. In some places the cultural norm is far more collectivist—perhaps it is the norm to live as one big family in a generational home with a "head of the family" who distributes roles and is the ultimate authority. In some countries, such as China and Korea, it is the legal responsibility of the adult child to provide for their parent when they reach old age and can no longer work, no matter what their relationship or their circumstances.

Cultural norms have an impact on how we feel about our relationships with our parents. For example, global news outlets—from major publications to tabloids—often condemn complicated parental or family relationships. Just take the recent notable estrangements in pop culture, such as Prince Harry and the other members of the royal family. Media outlets have rejoiced in blaming his decisions on his spouse, amplifying the rhetoric that he's selfish and immature for opening up about his childhood experiences (which we know were extremely privileged but also traumatic), and generally painting him as an unworthy son. There is a history of media fascination with stars who don't have positive relationships with their parents—Angelina Jolie, Macaulay Culkin, Drew Barrymore and Eminem, for example—often labeling them "difficult" or "spoiled" and sensationalizing their trauma and experiences. It's worth remembering that this was the same language used to discredit women in the 1950s who wanted to divorce their abusive spouses—selfish, spoiled, uncompromising, no respect for the family unit. This becomes more prominent when we add in our own children; suddenly, we're not just the spoiled child but the villain for not allowing the sweet, innocent granny or gramps to see *their* grandchild. Indeed the media, literature and society have a role to play in how we view grandparents and their role in a child's life; rarely do we see them portrayed as someone who it's necessary to protect our children from, other than in the most extreme circumstances.

Regardless of your circumstances, I want you to remember this:

No one is entitled to you because they are titled to you.

Regardless of what your title is to another person—mom, dad, brother, sister, grandma, spouse—you are not entitled to remain in that person's life if they choose not to have contact with you. You're not selfish or spoiled for choosing to protect yourself from someone who causes you harm, and you don't owe anyone a role in your life—especially if that role is going to be detrimental to your overall wellbeing. As parents, especially cycle breakers who are fighting against a parent who won't put in the work or change their toxic behavior, it's our job to protect our children and decide what is and isn't detrimental to them.

Ever since I became a mother, I have known on some level that I didn't want my children to be subjected to the same toxic behaviors I was by my mother. When we realized that, unbeknownst to us, my mother was repeating the same patterns of behavior with our son, we knew we had to act. It is my role as their parent, in collaboration with their dad, to protect them when I feel they may be in harm's way. That doesn't mean you are weaponizing a child. If you feel that they will be subjected to hearing you badmouthed, asked to keep secrets or treated in any of the ways you were, then you are absolutely within your rights (and it is your responsibility) to protect them from that. Or you might feel that they won't experience these things, and that your parent is a wholly different person with them; you may see a relationship that you think is safe and worth encouraging for your child's sake. That is where boundaries will come in, and we will explore these in the next chapter.

Chapter 4

Boundaries

You *are* entitled to set boundaries. Boundaries are something that you will find we will discuss often throughout the book, as they are an essential part of maintaining any healthy relationship, including the one that you have with yourself and your children. A very basic way of understanding boundaries is that they help you to work out what you are comfortable with and what kind of treatment you will accept. **Boundaries are always about** *you*—they don't seek to control or manipulate another person. Boundaries are especially important for cycle breakers, who are often conditioned as children to believe that setting boundaries with parents is somehow inherently wrong, disloyal or disrespectful. As discussed in the previous chapter regarding how we view estrangements, this is prevalent across cultures but can be especially present in more collectivist cultures where there is a perceived "head of the family" who makes choices for all. But we must set boundaries within our relationships, not just for ourselves but for others too, and especially as parents. Setting boundaries, modeling healthy boundaries and teaching your children to set boundaries *matter*.

An easy way to break down or communicate a boundary is to remember that it will always:

1. have an "I" statement or an expression that shares how you feel about something/what you are experiencing; and
2. express how you would prefer the person to behave toward you and outline what course of action you will take if they choose to continue with their current behavior.

For example, "**I feel** frustrated when you come over unannounced, and if you choose to continue to do this, **I will** not be answering the door to you," or, "**It doesn't work for me** to see you on a weekend because we are at various clubs for the kids. **I won't be available** then, but **I'm happy to see you during the week**."

It's important to remember that boundaries are personal—the above examples may deeply resonate with you, but you may also read them and feel they're harsh and unnecessary. Neither feeling is right or wrong, it's simply that different people have different boundaries, and that's often where our struggles in understanding each other lie. As for struggling with setting boundaries, think of it as another muscle you need to flex—the more you do, the stronger it will become. If you read the above and felt it was too much for you to start with, you can try using the traffic light system recommended by Melissa Urban in her book *The Book of Boundaries* to help you create boundaries with family when there have never been any, which is outlined below:

Green (gently raising the issue and how it impacts you, gently outlining your expectations moving forward)

This might sound like: "Mom, I know it comes from a good place, but **I feel really upset and frustrated** that you've given my child this food when I've asked you not to, and told them to keep that from me. We don't want them to keep secrets. **Please respect our wishes as parents and don't do it again. I really enjoy that they spend time with you, and I don't want to have to stop doing that because I can't trust you.**"

Yellow (reminding them of the issue, reinforcing how you feel and how you will react)

This might sound like: "Mom, I told you giving my child food we have asked you not to and telling them to hide it from me **makes me feel really upset and frustrated.** It damages our relationship when you do this, and **if it happens again, I will not leave them with you.**"

Red (reinforcing the boundary and acting on it)

This might sound like: "**I've explained what will happen** if you keep feeding my child food I've asked you not to and encouraging them to lie to us. Therefore, **I will no longer be leaving them with you.**" *And act on it.*

This system can be really effective for setting boundaries with people who don't respond well to them and who you want to maintain a relationship with, or if you are anxious about setting boundaries for the first time. A few notes on this traffic light system and boundaries in general:

- Acknowledging good intentions only happens in the green phase, because something can't be done with good intentions if you've been informed that it is harmful.
- It doesn't work if you stay stuck in one phase or you don't follow through with the action, so don't make statements that you don't think you will follow through with.
- You may find it quite triggering to see this "three-strike" style system if you had an authoritarian parent. It's OK if this doesn't work for you. You might choose to reframe this way of setting boundaries as giving your parent grace, a chance to grow and develop awareness, or perhaps it suits you better to think of the process in steps like set—remind—act.

Cycle breaker's toolkit: The Four Tendencies by Gretchen Rubin

I first learned about podcaster and writer Gretchen Rubin's Four Tendencies framework from Melissa Urban's brilliant book *The Book of Boundaries*. Since then I've not only read the book, but I've also taken all the quizzes (which you will find in the resources section). The Four Tendencies framework looks at how we respond to external and internal expectations—that is, the expectations placed on us from outside, and the expectations we place on ourselves. This gives us a deeper understanding of the personality type we have and can help us to understand how and why we feel the way we do around boundaries (both setting them and having them set with us).

Rubin determined that there are four main "tendencies." These are:

- **Upholders**—these people respond really well to outer and inner expectations. If they say they are going to do something (like stick to a new routine), then they will. Equally, if you ask them to do something, then they won't have an issue just . . . doing it.
- **Questioners**—these people will question all expectations, but if you can convince them something is the right option, they will do it. All outer expectations become inner ones to them, because they have to think through whether or not *they* want to do the thing, whether it's worth it to them.
- **Obligers**—these people are the ones we'd typically call "people-pleasers." They meet everyone's expectations of them . . . but not their own. What this means is that they often struggle to do the things they want and need some kind of external accountability or force to drive them.
- **Rebels**—these people resist all expectations, whether they are coming from inside or outside. They want freedom to do things, and any pressure will feel like a no go, even if it's internal pressure.

Can you identify with any of these personality types? If you're not sure, I strongly recommend giving the quiz a try. It's important to remember that no one type is better than another, it's simply about how we react to internal and external pressures. I think it's also important to note that we can have a natural inclination toward these personality types, but trauma can also have a big role to play in how we grow.

Cycle breaker's toolkit: Boundaries exercise

This exercise is a great way to reshape how you view your ability to set boundaries and perhaps to see where you would like to set more or uphold them more firmly.

Take an ordinary day in your life (or you may wish to make this a week, if it suits you better!) and consider all the things that happened. Start from when you woke up (maybe you've noticed you feel sluggish in the morning so you've told yourself you won't hit snooze anymore—did you hit snooze? If you didn't, that's a self-boundary!) and end when you closed your eyes (did you decide to turn off Netflix instead of watching just one more episode because you knew you'd be tired and you'd promised yourself you would get an early night? Also a boundary with yourself!).

Remember, a boundary is the limit you set. It marks out what *you* find acceptable. It can be with yourself, at work, in a romantic relationship, in a friendship, with family and even with strangers.

Examples of boundaries I've set today:

- I told my son he had to have a proper breakfast. He wanted a piece of leftover garlic bread and some cake for his breakfast. I gave him options that I (as the adult in the house) thought were acceptable and told him I would make sure he had a piece of both for dinner this evening. My boundary was that we eat nutritional breakfasts as a family.

- I needed some groceries from the local supermarket and chose to walk instead of hop in the car. I like to speed through errands and feel as productive as possible through the day, but always taking the car leaves very little opportunity in my day for the movement I know makes me feel better and helps my mental health. My boundary was with myself here—to care for my physical and mental health by getting some movement into my day even though my instinct was to take the speediest option.
- I told a colleague that I wouldn't be able to fulfill their request by the end of the day as it was too last minute. My boundary was with my colleague and myself to respect my time.
- I didn't allow my client session to run over. My boundary was with my client and myself; it was about respecting my time and theirs.
- I didn't answer work emails after 5pm. My boundary was with work and about setting clear time expectations.

Sometimes, the things that we overlook are examples of where we are setting boundaries without even realizing, but these are the areas where we can learn about ourselves *and* that we can pull on for strength during those bigger boundary moments.

So . . .

- What boundaries did you set? Who were they with?
- Where did you feel the most comfortable and confident setting boundaries?
- Was there a time that you didn't set a boundary but, looking back, you think one was necessary? (Mine is the snooze button!)

Setting the ultimate boundary and asking for no contact

One of the things I have noticed when working with clients is a lack of closure when it comes to a lot of dysfunctional family relationships. This is often the case when a big argument has caused a sudden estrangement, or when low contact is gently fizzling into less and less contact without anyone explicitly stating that the relationship is over. If you find yourself in a position where you are struggling with closure, or you want to create a boundary that says you no longer want contact, I strongly recommend trying the empty chair exercise outlined on page 56, or heading to the end of our first section and following the guided journaling steps, specifically the letter writing.

Once you have done that, if you feel it's helpful to you to have some kind of communication that draws a line under your relationship, you may wish to write a letter or email to your parent and let them know that you no longer wish to have contact and would ask them to respect your wishes. Keep the letter or email neutral, and avoid the temptation to over-explain. You might want to include all of your reasons, moments from your childhood that have caused you harm and damaged the relationship, but I would invite you to ask yourself the following: will it be heard and received with openness by your parent or parents? If you're seeking validation for your feelings and an acknowledgment of the way you have been treated, do your parents have the capacity to offer you that, or are you opening yourself to deeper hurt and invalidation? This is where the empty chair exercise or private letter can be really useful, in allowing you to release those feelings without subjecting yourself to further harm. You may feel that writing a letter or email to your parents to set that boundary of no contact doesn't help you, and that's an equally valid choice. In the case of no contact, there is no correct way to navigate social media or contact via phones/emails; however, I would spend a bit of time reflecting on how you would feel if you received an email or text from your parent(s). How would you feel to see them on social media with your siblings or posting a meme about always loving their child? If that feels triggering for you, you may wish to take steps to mitigate that by blocking them online and their number.

For many clients, there is a deep-seated fear that their parent will turn up on the doorstep, especially if they have been physically abusive in the past. In some cases this does happen, but I would urge you to remember that if you wouldn't tolerate that behavior from a partner or friend, you don't have to tolerate it from a parent, and you are within your rights to contact appropriate authorities if needed, or simply refuse to open the door. This can be a deeply stressful situation, especially if children are involved, and we will talk about how to parent in these situations later in the book.

I am a big believer in creating your own closure through methods like the empty chair exercise or working toward a place of acceptance. I think sometimes we hide behind a desire for closure because we're not 100 percent confident in our decision or we *hope* (that pesky emotion that wreaks havoc amidst a family filled with hurt and dysfunction) that our parent will change their behavior, be accountable for their mistakes and validate us. Sometimes, that isn't going to happen. And that truly sucks. There is no amount of gentle coaching or "therapy speak" that can soften the blow of a parent who simply won't meet you part way and help you rebuild or try to repair the relationship that could have been.

As I mentioned before, as we go through this book together, we will discuss boundaries often because they are fundamental to cycle-breaking parenting. I feel it's important to note here that boundaries are an uncomfortable part of life—even the most seasoned boundary setter will feel that pinch of discomfort and awkwardness when setting a new boundary, especially if it's in response to someone crossing one. When you have grown up in a dysfunctional family, setting boundaries is far from second nature and it's OK if you find yourself struggling. For many, learning to set boundaries is a process that includes feeling empowered and free but also guilty and overwhelmed. Be kind to yourself and remember that you are learning a whole new way of relating to others (and yourself) and it's OK for it to be tough. You don't have to be perfect at boundary setting either—I remember many occasions where I would set them, be completely sure about them and then backtrack when it became too uncomfortable or guilt-inducing. What matters is that you get to a place where you feel confident and happier in yourself.

Later on in the book, we will also talk about setting boundaries with your children, as well as teaching them to set boundaries (and how to cope when they do it with you—because it is an experience like no other, with so many contradictory feelings and emotions). I find that one of the most challenging aspects of being a cycle-breaking parent and teaching your children to set boundaries with everyone, including you, is that it pushes against every narrative you have ever been given. It's not uncommon for a client to say to me about their child, "I just keep thinking they are so rude, but if they set boundaries as an adult I wouldn't have a problem. It's *so* hard!" You're not alone, it's completely reasonable to find that the contrast between your chosen style of parenting and your experience of being parented leaves you feeling at odds. You will get there.

Chapter 5

Debt mindset vs. gratitude

Growing up within a dysfunctional family set-up means you've more than likely heard phrases like "after all I've done for you," or been told you are ungrateful in some capacity or other. I want to address the difference between debt mindset and gratitude, and why so many parents entangle the two.

Where does debt mindset come from?

In short, it comes from generational trauma and the sense of entitlement that is so common in dysfunctional parent–child relationships. Many of our parents were raised with the view that children should be seen, not heard, that they didn't have emotional needs (we only accepted they did in wider psychology from the 1950s onwards), and that meeting anything beyond the basic requirements for food and shelter meant that you were a "good parent," especially if you were authoritarian and kept discipline at the fore. This is especially relevant in understanding why debt mindset occurs. Many of those parents will have continued this style of parenting, or perhaps they chose to swing completely the opposite way and became permissive parents who treated their children more as friends and raised them without boundaries.

For many older generations, becoming a parent wasn't so much a "want" as an expectation—life followed one path and that path was something along the lines of: go to school, get a job, find a partner of the opposite gender, get married and have kids. People who didn't follow this path were othered and seen as somehow defective—especially women (who still are in many ways, though *some* progress has been made). Sacrifice was written into the very fabric of parenting—especially for women. Sacrifice your career, sacrifice your body, sacrifice your money . . . sacrifice . . . and all without really ever being given the autonomy to consider if having children was something you *wanted.*

Having children *is* life changing. Some of us enter into it and find that it differs from our expectations, while some may never have considered that having children is optional, but rather viewed it as a natural progression of life. Either scenario can cause resentment or a sense of being owed by this tiny human who you have made (or at least perceive to have made) sacrifices for. I spent a lot of my teens and younger adult years telling anyone who would listen how much I "owed" my mother. I would list my achievements and credit her, point out all the failings of my father and how she was the only reason I achieved anything. And I truly believed it. This rhetoric I was spouting came, in part, from societal attitudes toward parents, and how we must be grateful for their "sacrifices," but also from my mother herself—something I never noticed until I started to question the narrative of "owing" a parent.

Those questions came to the fore when I had my own children and realized how unhealthy this attitude was. I didn't want my children to feel they *owed* me or to consider their achievements mine by proxy. Growing up, my sense of being indebted to my mother was subtly woven into the fabric of my being, and I had constant glimpses into how she felt about motherhood. My childhood was littered with phrases we've probably all heard, like "after all I do for you!" or tales of the career opportunities missed and sacrifices made.

My personal experience was also jumbled with soft words: "You don't owe me anything, darling, I just want you to be happy," or, "Oh, but it was so worth it for you." Perhaps yours was too, which can be deeply confusing when you're constantly being given the message that you do, in fact, owe a lot merely for existing. This is a common tactic for emotionally abusive parents, who raise their children to experience life with fear, obligation and guilt (FOG) as their driving emotions, which impacts everything they do and the decisions that they make. These feelings are weaponized against us by toxic parents, allowing the parent to remain in control, prioritizing their feelings and needs above the child's and encouraging them to do the same. As we grow older, we continue to feel **obliged** to sit in a space where we prioritize our parent's demands and feelings above our own, and we feel **guilt** if we don't and **fear** of the abandonment or rejection our childlike selves remember. FOG becomes the driver in our internal vehicle, constantly informing our behaviors to protect us from the shame we were taught in childhood. In chapter 2 we talked about how trauma responses—fight, flight, fawn and freeze—may present for us in relationships or daily life. These are our *survival* responses, built from a constant ringing of our internal alarm—fear—that tells us our primary drive to survive (emotionally or physically) is at risk. It was only in my adulthood, and more specifically after I had children, that I started to reflect on these mixed messages and the way in which my mother's actions supported her sense of feeling owed. As I started to develop my own sense of self and step into my autonomy as an adult, the sense of entitlement, resentment and being owed became startlingly apparent— which in my experience is a common theme for many adults who grew up in dysfunction.

You might be wondering where gratitude fits into all of this. It's important to acknowledge that gratitude is never owed, nor is it to the detriment or sacrifice of yourself. You cannot force someone to feel authentic gratitude, and in addition, two truths can coexist. You can simultaneously acknowledge the things that your parents did right, and feel grateful to them for those things, while holding them accountable for the mistakes they made. You can see the hard work that they put into raising you, if they did, while also feeling joy in and ownership of your own achievements. It's important as cycle-breaking parents that we recognize and accept that children don't "owe" parents anything, including a relationship: acknowledging that and instilling that mindset in our children doesn't mean that they won't be able to show gratitude or will grow into "spoiled brats," as we're so often told. Gratitude has some wonderful benefits for our spiritual and emotional wellbeing, but for a lot of cycle breakers that is overshadowed by a narrative that confuses debt mindset and tells us that gratitude must involve sacrifice or be to the detriment of ourselves.

What came up for you in this section? Do you find yourself

saying things like "after all I do for you?" to your own children and passing on some of that debt mindset, if you were raised with it yourself? How do you feel about the concept of not "owing" a parent for raising you—can you reframe the narrative you have been given and view your parent as someone simply fulfilling the responsibilities and obligations they took on when they chose to have a child and raise them? It can be complicated for many people, so take your time and reflect on those questions; you might wish to use them as journal prompts.

If you find yourself in a cycle of creating a debt mindset with your children, don't panic. As parents, we are *all* parenting with the blueprint we have been given. For some of us, that blueprint is one we know we don't want to follow, but it's all we've got. We are slowly building up the tools in our toolkit, and in reading this book we are strengthening them together. But the truth is that we will find our parents popping out of us from time to time. Being mindful of this is a huge part of the changes we seek to make. If you do find yourself feeling owed by your child, now is the time to challenge that feeling. Mistakes are an inevitable part of parenting, and cycle-breaking parenting is no exception. Being mindful of our mistakes, holding ourselves accountable and working hard to address our own traumas is where the difference between you and your parents lies.

Journaling pages

Let's jump right in. Find somewhere quiet, plant your feet on the ground and take a moment to connect with your breath. Take a deep breath in, and as you release that breath, allow your shoulders to relax, unclench your jaw and feel your muscles relax.

- Head back to Maslow's Hierarchy of Needs on page 35 and take a look at the basic needs. I'd like you to think back to your childhood, and if you don't have solid memories of it, focus on the feelings that arise when you consider the things in the pyramid. How do you feel about how your needs were met? Does it surprise you to see physical touch at the very lowest level of the pyramid? Perhaps you didn't think of play as a "need" before? I'd like you to jot down in your journal or on a piece of paper what you feel you didn't receive from your parents. Take your time as this can bring up some deep, uncomfortable feelings. When you have done that, I would like you to take a look at your list and write down how *you* as an adult will fulfill those needs for yourself now.

- Write a letter to your parent(s)—what do you want to say that you have never felt you could?

- Close your eyes (or if you prefer, lower your eyes to the floor) and visualize your younger self. This can be you at any stage of childhood or young adult life, and you can do this exercise as many times as you feel you need to to address your younger self at different stages. Once you have a clear idea of that younger self, think of what it is that you would tell that younger self as your self now. What is it that you feel they needed, and perhaps still need, to hear? Jot that down.

Section 2

Shame, boundaries and family reactions

In section 2, we're stepping forward in your journey of cycle-breaking parenting and starting to look more closely at you in the now as a person and a parent. We'll discuss how your experiences with your parents impact how you view yourself and your children, and how to navigate shame, stigma and negativity to move into a space where you can meet your child in a more grounded way.

We will discuss how to talk to your child about family trauma and estrangement in an age-appropriate way, and support them if and when they ask tough questions like, "Why don't we see Grandma anymore?" or "Why is Grandad so mean?"

Take a deep, grounding breath and let's begin . . .

Chapter 6

Shame and stigma surrounding estrangement and toxic family

Stigma can hugely influence our choices around estrangement and toxic family dynamics. Even within some heavily influential works dedicated to understanding our intergenerational inheritance of trauma and epigenetics, such as Mark Wolynn's *It Didn't Start with You*, there is an undercurrent that *all should be forgiven* when it comes to our parents and their treatment of us, simply because they are a part of our lineage.

Stigma will always be present within the uncomfortable topics of trauma and abuse, even with the work that we are doing and the strides that we have taken over the last few decades to open up the conversation surrounding abuse. If it makes us uncomfortable, we are predisposed to shy away from it, and nothing will make a person more uncomfortable than having a light shone on the skeletons in their family closet. And so we pass down the message from generation to generation that we don't talk about it, and when we hear someone else talking about their experiences, it hits a nerve and makes us uncomfortable. This stigma comes from inherited shame that runs like a thread through our lineage and society.

The likelihood is that you have heard phrases like "don't air your dirty laundry" or "it's family business" when it comes to familial disputes. These may even have been said to shut your partner out, creating a "just family" rhetoric that isolates you from the family you have chosen and created.

In all my time speaking to people who are either estranged or navigating toxic family dynamics, I have yet to hear these types of phrases used in a positive manner that doesn't either isolate or hide something that needs challenging in order to reach a healthier and more fulfilling relationship. I think that's worth sitting with for a minute. Have you ever known someone be told not to air the "family laundry" for positive reasons? It all links back to shame and stigma.

Stigma and shame sit both outside the family unit and within it. Many families operate with a "keep calm and carry on" attitude, using phrases like "Ah, that's just the way he/she is!" to excuse or dismiss concerns around a volatile parent. Many adult children of family dysfunction report being told by their "good" parent or a trusted adult within the family circle, either as a child after an incident or as an adult who has tried to raise concerns, "Look, it's just the way they are," or, "I know Mom/Dad can be difficult, but they are under a lot of stress with work. Better to just stay out of the way, OK?" We would rather dismiss and bury our heads than address the *shame* of family dysfunction.

Perhaps you're thinking, "OK, Harriet, that's great, but what do we do about that shame and stigma?" Well, we keep airing it, we keep talking and we keep stepping forward for ourselves. I'm not suggesting you write a page-long rant and post it on Facebook, but do show up for yourself and keep challenging the narrative that you have been set, even if you're not directly challenging your parents. I routinely have conversations with clients and people within my online community that go along the lines of, "I don't see my parents often. My relationship with my mom/dad is awful, but I've always really loved them and I don't want to never speak to them again. But when I try to talk to them about the way I feel, I'm shut down so quickly. It is literally like watching a cloud descend over their face! Since I've had children, I can't stop thinking about how they have never showed up for me. Even when Mom/Dad wasn't being awful, they just . . . didn't."

I want to note two things about experiences like this. Firstly, from a shame point of view, it's deeply difficult to continue to have invalidating and dismissive conversations with people who simply will not address their trauma or acknowledge your lived experience. For them, it's shame and an unwillingness or inability to step into a place of discomfort and make the necessary changes, but for you, it compounds self-shame and encourages you to take part in your own gaslighting by making you wonder, "Was it really that bad? Am I dramatic or the problem?"

Secondly, so often when we become parents ourselves, we start to reframe how we viewed both our parents. We often develop an awareness that the person we relied on as our "good parent," the one we told ourselves was our ally or our support against the overtly difficult parent, actually let us down too. This parent, who stood on the sidelines or perhaps dismissed our concerns and took part in upholding the toxic family dynamic, is what we would call an "enabler."

Sometimes this realization can be deeply traumatic in itself, and brings up feelings of anger and betrayal, making us reconsider our entire relationship with this "good parent," and leaving us wanting to ask, "Why didn't you step up for me? I'm your child, where was your love and support for *me*?"

If this is a realization you're just coming to now as you read this section of the book, I'd like you to pause and check in with yourself. Place your feet on the floor and take a few slow, deep breaths to ground yourself:

- in for a count of four
- hold for four
- out for a count of six

Repeat this a few times, ideally for a period of three to five minutes until you feel yourself relax; notice the sensation of your feet planted on the floor and the way your socks or the carpet feels.

Take a break if you need to and refer to the five senses grounding exercise (page 95) for calming your nerves or helping work through anxiety or overwhelming emotions.

I don't particularly want to focus on your parent(s) and why they have acted the way they have—after all, this book is about *you*—but in order to break cycles, it is important to cultivate understanding.

There are a million and one reasons why your parents may behave the way they do and exhibit some of the toxic behaviors we talked about earlier in the book, or turn a blind eye to those behaviors if they are the enabler. The common theme amongst all of these reasons is trauma—specifically your parent's own lived experience of trauma and inherited trauma. I want to really underline one point here. Our parents may be the way they are because of genetics or their own lived experiences, *but that doesn't excuse their behavior.* There is a real power in understanding and being able to step back from the enabling parent in the example above and say, "I can see that they didn't step forward for me because they were raised to believe mental health wasn't a real thing," or, "They were looking for an easy life because they witnessed a lot of struggles between their own parents growing up," or, "They are the way they are because they've always been shown people-pleasing tendencies." While the power lies in understanding the potential life experiences and trauma that have led us to the place we're at, that doesn't mean we have to accept the behavior or go without challenging it. Nor do we have to forgive.

So let's dig into your shame and the family story you may have been a part of (or disrupted and been cast aside because of). One of the things I found the most healing when I worked to understand the stigma and shame surrounding estrangement and toxic family dynamics was the concept of acceptance and understanding vs. forgiveness. As Dr. Mariel Buqué said in her brilliant book *Break the Cycle*, you don't have to forgive to heal.

Humans are complex beings, and we can simultaneously look at our parent's behaviors and say, "Yes, I understand why you have done the things you have done, I accept that this happened to me . . . and I choose not to forgive you." Does that sound odd to you? Many self-help books will preach the importance of forgiveness as an unattainable point of true healing, no matter how vile or traumatic your experiences have been. The theory is often that without forgiveness we simply harbor resentment and anger, which will pollute our being and leave us stuck and unable to move forward. But I, and many trauma-led professionals, can tell you that that's absolutely untrue, and it can in fact be detrimental to your own healing to force something you don't feel. Perhaps you do feel forgiveness is a part of your journey, and that's OK too, but what I really want to emphasize is that it shouldn't be a goal you set yourself just because a guru tells you you must or else you won't break free of toxic cycles.

In this chapter I will offer you the goal of understanding and acceptance. Understanding of how your parents became the way they are and why they acted the way they did. Acceptance that these things happened to you. Acceptance that it was unfair and the burden of changing the trauma legacy of your own family lies with you. Acceptance that you can't go back and change it. Acceptance of what is within the realm of your control and responsibility as an adult now. Acceptance that your parenting journey may be made that bit harder by the lack of a healthy blueprint and, finally, a challenge to move forward with your life in the knowledge that you don't have to force forgiveness if you don't feel it's right for you, and you can heal your own shame and family traumas. You can be the parent you needed for yourself and your child, and by doing simple things like reading this book and working on your own trauma in a way your parents chose not to, you're already on the path.

Cycle breaker's toolkit:
Five senses grounding exercise

This is an extremely useful tool when you are working through feelings of anxiety and panic, which are often brought on or inflamed by suppressed shame. It's simple and easy, and also works really well for children.

Start by focusing on taking deep, steady breaths in through the nose and out through the mouth. You might want to do this for a count of four in and seven out.

Look around you and name (aloud or in your head):

- five things you can see
- four things you can feel
- three things you can hear
- two things you can smell
- one thing you can taste

The purpose of this exercise is to bring you back to the here and now, and help you feel present in your body and calm your anxiety. Our minds can only focus on so many things at once, so if you're busy finding out what you can see, feel, hear, smell and taste, your senses will take over and your brain will focus on them instead of your triggers.

Chapter 7

Dealing with negativity

Negativity is something that you will no doubt come up against in your life on a daily basis, but how we manage it is entirely dependent on who we are and what has shaped us, the type of negativity we face and who we are facing it from.

Studies suggest that many people who experienced traumatic childhoods, especially when they had to play the role of parent from a young age, are exceptionally efficient and calm in the face of a crisis or when dealing with someone else's trauma or difficult events. It's no coincidence that many of us move into helping professions—you do what you know. Yet there is a difference between a crisis where a level of detachment comes naturally, and one where your parent makes snide remarks about how you choose to deal with your toddler, or worse still, when they try to take over and "discipline" them how they see fit. *That* type of negative experience isn't so easily met with a cool, calm detachment that may need to be worked through later; it's more often than not met with one of the autonomic trauma responses—fight, flight, fawn or freeze. The same is true when you experience smear campaigns at the hands of a narcissistic parent, or when family members pressure you or refuse to speak to you because you have set boundaries and they view it as cruel, or a million and one other experiences.

So, how do we deal with these moments of negativity? Let's break it down.

Dealing with negativity about your relationship (or lack thereof) with your parents

Negativity about your relationship with your parents is always going to be tough. Perhaps it comes from a well-meaning family friend who can't understand why you have limited or no contact—after all, they are "so nice." Or maybe it comes from smear campaigns directed by your parent, painting you as the "bad guy" and creating a deliberate divide between you and others. Regardless, it's . . . tough.

Who and where you're going to face negativity from will be unique to your circumstances. Clients of mine have faced it from the other parent, step-parents, their parent's ex-partner, family friends, siblings, extended family, partners, strangers, work colleagues, their own children and more. It can come from all angles, sometimes expected and sometimes totally out of the blue. Worst of all, it can and often does come from an internal place within us—a lingering guilt over a relationship we have felt responsible for our entire lives, or perhaps a fear that we will have to live with regret, that we're being unreasonable or that our own children will choose to distance themselves from us and we will make more mistakes than we realize.

There is one common denominator in dealing with

negativity when it comes to your relationship with your parents, and that is **boundaries**. A boundary is a set of limits around how you want to be treated and what you will and won't be comfortable tolerating. Let's flick back to the very beginning of the book and my retelling of the woman at the takeout counter asking me repeatedly if I had contacted my mom and "extended the olive branch." Though somewhat blunt and haphazard, when I eventually lost my patience and told her to stop asking, that was me setting a boundary. For me, someone pressing me to make contact or "fix" things with my mom, especially a stranger in a bizarre situation, went way beyond my personal boundaries, and it's our responsibility to vocalize those boundaries for ourselves (and sometimes for our kids too).

So how do you know you need to set a boundary?

Think of a situation in which you have felt uncomfortable—that right there is a pretty big indicator that a boundary is being overstepped or ignored, or that you need to set one. It might be that you have asked for no contact from your parents, and your sibling is chatting away about what they did with Mom that weekend and how much Mom misses you. It might be the work colleague who feels the need to tell you how much they miss their parent who has passed away, and that you should just appreciate your father, he's doing his best. Or maybe it's the woman at the takeout counter you barely know asking you to reach out to your parent. Whatever it is, it's likely that if it's making you feel uncomfortable, it's time to step forward for yourself and say so.

How does it feel to think about doing that? Even more uncomfortable? Anxiety inducing? The truth is, boundaries *are* uncomfortable. They are rarely easy to set and often the closer you are with a person, the harder it is to do.

When you are considering setting a boundary surrounding someone's negative response to your relationship with your parents, there are a few questions it can be helpful to ask:

- Do I value this person, their input and my relationship with them?
- What part of me am I betraying or sacrificing if I allow things to continue this way?
- If I am now the "parent" for myself, what do I need?

Let's work backwards . . .

If I am now the "parent" for myself, what do I need?

It might feel like an odd concept, being the parent for yourself. Hopefully by now you're realizing that a big part of cycle-breaking parenting lies in reparenting yourself first. That is why we spent so much of section 1 looking back at your own experiences. As adults we make the decisions, we're the ones in the metaphorical driver's seat of our lives, and, sticking with the driver analogy, if the oil light comes on (i.e. we're uncomfortable), we are responsible for fixing the issue.

"Reparenting" is a term that comes up quite a lot in the cycle-breaking sphere, as a way to explain that what we're doing as adults is not only taking care of ourselves and being responsible, functioning members of society, but also taking care of our inner child who didn't learn these skills in early life, or learned that taking care of others mattered far more than we did. Asking yourself "What do I need?" when you notice those feelings of discomfort in a situation is a key part of parenting yourself, and learning to set boundaries. It's not just about recognizing what you need, but also about getting curious about where these feelings are coming from and why you're experiencing them.

What part of me am I betraying or sacrificing if I allow things to continue this way?

Often when a boundary is overstepped in adulthood or we don't set one at all, we have an odd feeling of self-betrayal. When we don't take charge of the situation to protect ourselves, we are transported back to those times—consciously or subconsciously—when we didn't have the ability to step forward and be our own advocate, when we were waiting for a parent or caregiver to do it for us. This feeling of betrayal might be lurking behind feelings of frustration, anger, irritation or defeat, and that is OK, but at the root for the majority of people there is self-betrayal. So, what part of you are you betraying when you don't set those boundaries or reaffirm them as needed? That would be your inner child, because, as we have already said, you're the parent now.

Do you find it weird to think of an "inner child"? I did. Initially there was a lot of cringing and eye rolling on my behalf; it seemed kooky and utterly weird to think of my "inner self," especially a child part. Then I swallowed my pride, chose to embrace it, and I can tell you that, beyond helping me heal and move forward, inner child work has been one of the dominant forces in helping me to connect with my own children *and* myself as a woman and mother.

Perhaps we can take the concept of an "inner child" and focus more on your memories of childhood and how they make you feel now (if you have any, and if you feel safe to look into them). If you struggle with memories of childhood, the inner child work exercises found in section 3 of this book can help too, as can embracing feeling memory, where you focus on the way your body feels when you think of events or people.

I have absolutely no memories of one of my uncles. I know he came to stay with us for a period of time when I was small, but when I try to remember that period, I have nothing but a blank space, some flashes of shadowy doorways and a feeling of deep-rooted fear. As an adult I learned that he suffered with schizophrenia and he would sleep for long periods through the day, which meant that, rather to the amusement of my mother, I was convinced he was a vampire. I also learned that he would often stop taking his medication and was eventually told he would need to leave because my mother found him standing over my bed in the middle of the night. When I think of this man now, I can't see his face or remember him, but my body remembers the way his presence made me feel. That is a *feeling memory*.

When working through trauma, we might feel that if we can't remember an event, we should ignore it, or if we prod too hard at the memory, it might well come back to light and we're not ready to face it. It's just as powerful to connect with your inner child over that feeling as it is to connect with them over a memory. You might be thinking, "But what can that tell me about my needs and boundaries now?" Sticking with my feeling memory surrounding my uncle, the knowledge of that helps me to connect to my inner child and get a sense of what she needs, to build a foundation of trust with myself in order to extend it to others. It allows me to sit with "little Harriet" in my mind and tell her that I will not allow her to be made to feel that scared again, that there are no "vampires" to fear, and I'm not going to let her down the way my mom let me down by allowing someone so unstable to stay with us.

What is a feeling memory you have from your childhood? How could you reassure your inner child to trust you to protect you both from that situation now? What would you do differently than your parent or caregiver? Perhaps here is a chance to tell your inner child about how you're doing things so differently with your child.

On a final note for the question of what part of yourself you are sacrificing: the likelihood is that this will vary drastically depending on you, your environment and the boundary being crossed, but I'm willing to venture that your overall mental wellness is being sacrificed to some degree. It might be that your physical health is being impacted, your sense of self, your autonomy, your self-respect, your feelings of self-worth and many other crucial things that help us to feel safe and centered as adults.

This is what I call the "keep-the-peace trade-off." When we get stuck in a keep-the-peace trade-off, we are constantly placing a hierarchy of value on integral parts of ourselves against not ruffling feathers, not causing a scene and (shocker) keeping the peace. We do all of this completely subconsciously, but every time we choose not to set or reaffirm our boundaries, we are saying, "My thoughts/feelings/self matter *less*," and we trade these in order to avoid the consequences of holding them at a higher value.

When you consider "keeping the peace," ask yourself: whose peace are you keeping? In some instances, it might be yours, but don't kid yourself—it's not *your* peace you're keeping if it makes you feel uncomfortable, miserable or stressed. When I talk about the "keep-the-peace trade-off" with clients, we find that simply having an awareness of when you're doing this makes all the difference. The simplest way to bring yourself into an awareness is to notice when a boundary is pushed or crossed (those feelings of discomfort), and to ask yourself: "Whose peace am I keeping here? What would I sacrifice to keep it? Is that sacrifice worth this trade?"

I think you'll be surprised how often the answer is no.

Do I value this person, their input and my relationship with them?

Remember I said that we often find it harder to set boundaries with people we're close to? You might well be a boundary-setting aficionado at this stage in your life, but I bet there is one person who you find it just a little bit harder or more awkward with. For many of us, this boils down to how much we care. Yes, we all like to be perceived well, but this is often on a surface level. When it comes to family, however, especially parents, we are hardwired to care deeply about how they view and treat us, and to want to build a connection with them (and while we "manage" this as adults who are capable of nuanced thought, the predisposition doesn't leave us). Setting boundaries with family will be different than setting boundaries in a work setting, which will be different than setting boundaries with a stranger standing too close to you on public transportation. The way in which we set a boundary will be impacted by how we feel about that relationship, how much we want to maintain connection and how much we value someone's input.

I had a client who came to me following a new estrangement from her mother to try and work through some of her experiences, build her confidence and navigate her new life. She had a really close relationship with her grandma, who would call her two or three times a week to "check in" and have a general chit-chat. My client deeply valued this relationship, it meant the world to her, and in her eyes Grandma had been the figure she needed growing up and whom she most looked up to. In the weeks following her estrangement from her mother, amidst angry emails from her siblings and raging voicemails from extended family she barely knew, her grandma started pushing her to reconcile. My client was devastated; the one relationship where she felt safe and enjoyed contact with her family of origin was now becoming a source of anxiety. She described spending their chats waiting for questions like "Have you spoken to your mom?", or being endlessly on guard. Despite setting what is arguably one of the hardest boundaries of all with her mother, replying to those angry emails with a firm message that she wouldn't tolerate being spoken to this way and blocking the numbers of extended family, she felt deep conflict over saying anything to her grandma because she cared so deeply and truly wanted to keep the relationship they had. This is a classic example of how tough it can be to set boundaries when faced with a desire to keep the relationship. I can't tell you how many clients come to me not because they are distressed over their toxic relationship with parents, but because they are struggling to come to terms with their sibling's reaction, or the loss of a relationship with their other parent.

I'm going to tell you what I tell my clients: if this relationship is what you believe it is, built on mutual respect and worthy of the value you're placing on it, you will have no problem when you set a boundary. In fact, it is in the interest of the relationship to set that boundary sooner rather than later, kindly, clearly and firmly. My client went back to her grandma and told her, "Nana, I love you, but please can you stop bringing up Mom? I am dealing with that, and while I know you might not approve, I need you to respect my choices." Grandma needed reminding a few times, but it was worth it to my client to maintain the relationship and eventually, slowly but surely, the anxiety that was haunting their relationship disappeared and they stayed connected.

We often think of boundaries as a one-stop fix, and once you have set one, anyone who doesn't respect it needs kicking to the curb. But that isn't real life. You can certainly do that, but sometimes we spend a bit of time in that yellow section of the traffic light system I mentioned on page 70, and we need to help our loved one learn *with* us.

Dealing with negativity surrounding your parenting

Regardless of your current relationship status with your parent, if you consider yourself someone who wishes to make changes to your legacy of generational trauma, then you are probably going to parent very differently from how you were parented. It might be that, despite relating to a lot of the issues we've shared so far, you consider yourself to have a relatively good relationship with your parent, but maybe they can't wrap their head around your "hippie parenting." Or you have a tolerant relationship with them, but face constant criticism that makes you doubt your parenting abilities. Or it could be a sibling, a family member or a partner who has a different parenting style than you, and this causes conflict.

As cycle breakers, we're often much more sensitive to criticism about our parenting abilities than other parents. How do you feel reading that? You might have some uncomfortable feelings bubble up when you read the word "sensitive," and I want to let you know that that is OK. People in dysfunctional families are often subjected to phrases that dismiss their experiences and feelings, such as "you're being too sensitive" or "you're dramatic," but I want to reassure you that being sensitive to criticism is perfectly normal, and not something that belittles you or your experience.

Is there anything more enraging than hearing your parent, who is at the root of your own trauma, telling you all the ways in which they feel you should parent *like them*? Way before I faced the toxicity of my relationship with my mother and was still enmeshed with her, I remember having an intense response to her telling me how she would do things with my son, and worse still, her taking over and trying to parent from underneath me. The rage felt palpable: this was my child, and I would *not* be raising him the way she had raised me, thank you very much.

It's not uncommon for a lot of estrangements or low-contact relationships to begin off the back of a parent trying to undermine your parenting. This is the point at which you have to be really firm with your boundaries, which is always going to ruffle some feathers. Ultimately *you* are choosing how to parent your child and absolutely no one, including your parents, has a say in how you forge that relationship. If you experience a negative response to your parenting, refer back to the traffic light system of boundaries again and let your parent know, gently but firmly, that you are not looking for their input here, you would like them to adapt their behavior when they are around your child and you won't tolerate them stepping on your toes. You don't owe anyone an explanation of why you're choosing to parent the way you are. If you're met with the classic, "Well, I'm just trying to help!", or you're dismissed or ignored, you can go ahead and affirm that boundary, following through with consequences if needed.

It's worth noting here that for some people it doesn't feel as simple as telling your parent that you parent differently, and then issuing a consequence if they keep interfering or ignoring you. It might be that you rely on that parent for childcare, or your child has a strong relationship with them and you don't want to remove them from their life. Even when we don't feel like it, there is always a choice. If you feel that your parent's derision of your parenting is negatively impacting your child or your relationship with your child, then you have a responsibility to take that seriously. Consider what alternative arrangements you could make for childcare, or how you could facilitate a relationship with clear, structured boundaries that meet with your parenting. I have a rule that when I'm there, I am the parent and what I say goes. I don't seek approval on my parenting style, and I make that clear, nor will I tolerate being questioned or undermined. That being said, when my children are just with their grandparents, things will be different, and that's OK. I don't expect their grandparents to follow my parenting style, but I do expect them to respect my boundaries, which might include things like not giving them sweets, or not discussing body size or shape around them.

When it comes to setting boundaries and dealing with negativity, we're often given the impression on social media that this will look a certain way, and if we don't set firm and unbendable boundaries, then we're letting ourselves down. In practice, boundaries often take time to establish, even with the most well-intentioned family members, but especially when there is dysfunction within the family unit. Only you can choose what your boundaries will look like and what you choose to do when someone doesn't respect them. In Sahaj Kohli's book *But What Will People Say?* she talks a lot about the reality of creating boundaries in different cultural dynamics. As we have touched on before, different cultures view parent–adult child relationships differently, and we risk alienating people from the conversation with a one-size-fits-all approach. Throughout her book, Kohli talks about how she has changed *her* behavior to protect herself and break the cycle of generational trauma in her family. I have to confess that when I first spoke to Kohli about this for my podcast, *Unfollowing Mum*, I felt uncomfortable at first. Should we be telling the victim in this scenario how to change things about themselves? I quickly realized that there is a fundamental difference here—that your wellbeing, not your parent's, is at the center of the choices you're making. If you choose not to cut contact with a parent for whatever reason, then you will need to make adaptions to your behavior to protect yourself. This might mean choosing not to acknowledge or rise to snide remarks, planning a schedule for phone calls with a parent so you can be prepared and have a time frame for the catch-up, or setting firm boundaries. The main point I came across in Kohli's book, and that I would like you to take away here, is that setting boundaries, breaking cycles and navigating generational trauma are complex. Adding to feelings of shame by berating or bullying yourself for not "doing it right" is only picking up the gauntlet from your parents.

Cycle breaker's toolkit: Exercise for getting in touch with what you need and thinking about setting boundaries

At different times, we may need to set boundaries in various parts of our lives. Here's an overview of the categories of boundaries to be mindful of:

- **Physical**—these include privacy, physical space and touch.
- **Time**—these include how long you spend with someone doing things, punctuality and expectations on your time.
- **Sexual**—these include discussions around sex, consent, jokes, pictures and suggestive language.
- **Emotional**—these include how you handle your own and others' emotional states, and to what extent you feel comfortable with others sharing their emotions with you or asking for emotions from you.
- **Material**—these include financial treatment, the sharing of assets and preferences around spending or your belongings/property.
- **Intellectual**—these include how you feel about sharing and handling information such as opinions, beliefs and ideas.

I'd like you to think about an individual you struggle to set boundaries with, or perhaps a situation in which you have been uncomfortable. What kind of boundaries would you say you need to set here? For example, perhaps it's a sibling who keeps pressuring you to talk to your parent. Looking at the boundary sections on the previous page, I feel this would be both emotional and intellectual:

- **Emotional:** I don't want to hear about my parent and I also don't feel comfortable with my sibling sharing information about me or my family with that parent. I can express this by saying clearly, "When we're together, I need you to stop talking about Mom/Dad, and I don't want anything I share with you to go back to them. If you can't respect that, it's going to be really difficult to spend time with you."
- **Intellectual:** I don't want to hear my sibling's thoughts on my choices or to have them belittled, so I can say, "Hey, I get it, you have a really different relationship with our parents, and I respect that. I'm asking you to respect my choices and I won't discuss them when we meet up."

Now, look again at the categories on the last page. Can you identify any areas where you need to set firmer boundaries? Jot down any scenarios that come to you.

Chapter 8

Talking to children about estrangement and toxic behavior from grandparents (or other family members)

One of the questions that crops up the most in sessions with clients surrounds navigating toxic family and children. I receive endless messages like, "How do I explain to my children why we're not seeing my mom/dad anymore?" Or, "My son has pointed out that Grandad is always really mean to me, and I don't know what to say!"

Navigating a toxic relationship with a parent is complicated, but when that parent has a relationship with your child and you have to be responsible for monitoring or cutting that contact too, it becomes a whole new level of difficult. Children are wonderfully curious beings, and they will ask the most awkward questions and offer us startlingly clarifying observations without any filter whatsoever.

I remember taking my children for a walk a few days after we asked my mom to move out of the annex we had built for her. When I asked her to leave, I had no intention of cutting contact completely; rather I hoped for a low-contact relationship that could be repaired with distance and boundaries. Looking back, I can see with crystal clarity how naive this hope was, but this is often the case with enmeshed families—the adult child asks for distance and a bit of autonomy and it's seen as such an insult that they are left with no choice but to completely step away. It was always my intention to have my mom in the children's lives—after all, she was their grandparent, and my only living parent. The day after my chat with Mom, my daughter had gone to sit with her in her yard and my mom took her to one side, at the age of five, and asked her to help her look for houses. This was so reminiscent of those early years I spent trying to regulate my mom's emotional state and act as her confidant, therapist and stand-in spouse. The wave of emotions that came up for me felt like a tsunami, totally unexpected and at the same time wholly predictable. It was retraumatizing in itself.

It was there and then that we realized we weren't going to be able to make this work the way I'd originally hoped.

Later that week came the walk, a moment in my life that feels defining and I will never forget. My eldest child turned to me as he was playing around the stream with his siblings and said, "Mom, what is happening with Maw Maw? Why isn't she allowed in the house? Why can't we see her?"

Three little faces were suddenly looking up at me, hoping for answers, and while I held on to our dog, I thought, "What the hell do I say?" I took a deep breath and replied, "Darlings, we have asked Maw Maw to live somewhere else because of the way she treats Mommy and Daddy. We aren't happy around each other. It's hard and it's sad, but just because we care about someone and they are family doesn't mean they can be unkind to us."

In this safe, neutral space the questions started to flow. "Will we ever see her again?" they asked. I gently replied, "I don't know. I had hoped to be able to go to see her at her new house, and spend time at Christmas, but she's very angry and at the moment I don't feel safe to be around her, and I don't feel safe for you to be around her. Maybe one day we will be able to do that." There was a sadness in receiving this response, especially for my eldest, who had been subjected to the same conditioning I had as a child, though to a lesser degree.

This chat was the first of many that gave me a real insight into how to speak to children about all kinds of difficult topics, not just estrangement or challenging family dynamics. After years of research, training and discussion with other professionals, I've come up with a solid framework for talking to children about difficult topics, and I'm going to share this with you here.

Avoid badmouthing

Badmouthing is so instinctual when a relationship ends badly. It's only natural to want people, including our children, to understand our version of events, and perhaps subconsciously we hope they will "side" with us. It also feels natural to tell them when someone's behavior is bad or dangerous in a bid to protect them; it's why we spend so much time telling them not to talk to strangers or warning them to stay away from children who aren't being kind. For the majority of people, especially those who have experienced gaslighting and been made to question their reality, there is a natural pull to over-explain and bring others "on our side." I'd just like to take a moment to sit with that—how does it feel to think of unconsciously wanting to create sides? Initially, I was hesitant about this; after all, I'd been raised by someone who always created division and expected me to be on *her* side, Team Mom. Was I just as bad, then, if I felt that pull? The reality is that we, as humans, want to feel supported and believed. We want the person we are explaining our situation to to be on our side, to validate that we are justified in our choices or at least understand and support us in making them. That is a natural feeling that we can't always escape or control. *But*, what we can control is how we allow that pull to shape our conversations with our children.

When we allow that need to be supported, to feel seen and understood, to overshadow our rational side, we fall into the trap of badmouthing. It's often unintentional; sometimes we skirt around what we're doing by telling ourselves we're simply telling the truth, and often we are, but we're not doing it in a way that serves our kids—we're serving ourselves and our need to be validated.

You might be thinking, "Er, OK, Harriet, but you just said you told your kids that their gran wasn't kind. Isn't that bad-mouthing?" In short, no. Had I said, "Maw Maw is really spiteful, she did XYZ to me and she is nasty," it would have carried a very different message to a child than, "Maw Maw isn't being kind," or, "Her behavior isn't kind." In focusing on her behavior/actions, and not over-explaining without them asking, I stayed neutral while offering a valid reason to set that boundary and step away. I was not defining a person, I was naming their behavior, which is a powerful distinction.

Sticking to neutral, minimal facts, avoiding labeling the person, and focusing on the action or the behavior is a powerful way to step away from badmouthing. In therapy and coaching we use the term "frame of reference" to describe what point of view we are looking at something from—the psychological equivalent of stepping into someone else's shoes. When we badmouth, we are in our frame of reference—all the hurt, all the anger and a whole host of big emotions get in the way. When we talk to our children as cycle breakers, we are in their frame of reference, considering their needs in asking that question.

Here are a few examples of the difference between badmouthing and staying neutral:

Badmouthing (from your frame of reference)	Neutral/cycle breaking (from your child's frame of reference)
Why aren't we going to see Grandad this weekend?	
Grandad is a nasty person. He's always been really cruel to me and bullies me every time we go over. You've seen him, haven't you? It's so awful. I've told him he has to stop and he doesn't even care enough to be nice just once, so we're not going anymore. I have to protect you from him.	Grandad doesn't act very kindly toward me and it's not OK for him to behave like that. I've asked him to stop, and he's chosen not to, so we won't be visiting this weekend. It's my job to protect us from that kind of behavior.
Why does Grandma call you names and pick on you when we see her?	
She's just really horrible. She's always been so nasty to me, even when I was a little girl she would call me names. She had a bad start in life and it's made her a spiteful, bitter person, so we have to be sorry for her.	You've noticed that, huh? I don't know why she does that, but it's not kind. Her mom and dad weren't always kind to her and that is what she grew up thinking was normal, but it's not. I can't control how she acts, but I can control how I act, and it's my job to stand up for myself, which is why sometimes we leave early.

Badmouthing (from your frame of reference)	Neutral/cycle breaking (from your child's frame of reference)
Grandma said you were a bad person but I am not supposed to tell you.	
She said what? She's totally out of order! I'm so angry, you wait until I see her! She's awful, I can't believe she would say that to you.	Oh dear, that's not good and certainly not something that should be said to you. Thank you for telling me, that was really smart and brave of you. I want you to know that it's not your responsibility to deal with this kind of thing. That is for grown-ups, and Grandma should know better. I will deal with it, OK?
Why don't you see your daddy?	
He's a nasty piece of work. He used to get drunk and hit me a lot when I was little, so we are better off without him.	My daddy was not kind to me when I was little. He used to hurt me, and that's not OK. (If you have an older child who has talked about addiction and substance abuse, you can add, "He had a lot of problems with addiction and while he needed help, that wasn't my job as his child. I have to protect myself and you.")

In all of these examples both the badmouthing and the cycle-breaking options are true, but can you see the way in which badmouthing centers us as a victim and encourages the child to step in and agree with us?

Am I badmouthing?

A really simple exercise that helps me to avoid badmouthing is to ask myself the following questions:

- Who does this answer serve? Is it to answer my child's question and help them understand, or is it to make me feel better?
- How would I feel hearing this? Am I being age appropriate here, and if not, how can I word what I want to share in this moment?

Being intentional and aware of how and why we are responding to our children the way we are is a huge part of cycle breaking.

I'd like to touch on talking to older kids here. I have a teenager, and I know that those of you reading this with older kids might be thinking, "Well, that's not helpful for me. My child hasn't said 'Mommy' in five years and we don't get gentle questions so much as angry statements. How the hell do I deal with that?!" Trust me, I relate. Communicating with teens can feel like a minefield—you're never quite sure if you've said the "wrong thing," and even when it felt like the right thing, they often stomp off to their rooms or sit in silence, and you're left thinking, "Did I do that wrong?"

For a lot of cycle breakers, their initial independence was squashed in their teen years; they weren't allowed to express opinions or have a sense of self beyond what suited their toxic parent. For others, it was the start of stepping away and challenging their parent, or perhaps it was when their parent's abuse started to really show. I've had many clients and people within my community report that their parent "seemed to love them" when they were little, but as soon as they got older, the interest faded and it was all about their younger siblings, who they were often made to care for. It's no wonder that being a parent to a teen is so tough, with all the hormones and the often subconscious trauma that comes up for us surrounding our own experiences, mingled with their moods and emotions and the natural pulling away from us as they grow into themselves.

The "no badmouthing" rule still applies here. Regardless of age—even in adulthood—badmouthing isn't a positive thing, but as we will see later in the book, communication needs to be age appropriate and honest. What that often means for older teens is co-regulating with them, holding space for their emotions and helping them work through them.

Let me give you an example of the kind of communication I've had with my teen recently.

We were walking back to the car after visiting a theme park during a school vacation and we got onto the topic of my childhood. My eldest is not a fan of rollercoasters, which is quite a contrast to his siblings, who often head off on the biggest and most terrifying rollercoaster they can find. Predictably, the kids were bickering about why rollercoasters were amazing and whether it was weird to like them or not. I remarked that they had never been for me either—in fact, I never really went on rollercoasters as a child because I had no one to go on with and my mom couldn't take me.

My son paused. "Why?" he blurted out. "Well," I said, "she

always told me that when she was younger she had a blood clot, and sometimes she would tell me about a broken neck, though honestly I'm not sure what was and wasn't true. Either way, she would always tell me she passed out when she went on the baby caterpillar ride with me when I was tiny, so she wouldn't risk anything else!" He didn't look at me as he declared, "Yeah well, she's a dickhead so she was probably just lying as usual."

In this moment a few things were going on. He was applying his own anger at the way she had treated him to my situation and those tough emotions had bubbled up, but he was also looking for a way to show me he was "on my side" and being protective. I could join in and fuel that fire, encouraging his (arguably valid) anger toward my mother, or I could tell him off for swearing or name calling, but what he needed was for me to hold the space without judgment. I replied, "That's true, she does sometimes lie and that's why it's so difficult to know what was and wasn't true. Lying sucks, it really hurts all those good foundations in a relationship, but that is why it matters to me so much that you can talk openly with me and your dad. Not everyone had that modeled to them." He frowned, grunted and moved on to talk about something else.

In this example, I didn't need to join in with badmouthing or saying anything negative about my mom, and it would have been counterproductive to defend her or try to change his perspective of her. She does lie from time to time. He's not yet old enough to have the conversation about the complex reasons why people lie or what constitutes a good or bad mother, or why someone behaves the way my mother does, but he is old enough that acknowledging what is in the room with us, so to speak, matters. Acknowledging that, yes, she lies, and then focusing on the behavior and why that matters in a more general pattern is important.

This brings me neatly to point two: open and honest communication at an age-appropriate level.

Open, honest communication (at an age-appropriate level)

There is a certain level of fear surrounding how much to tell your children, especially if you have been parentified and your parent has been an oversharer, continually placing you in the role of therapist or stand-in spouse. Toxic family dynamics aren't exactly an easy conversation topic at the best of times, but then talking about difficult topics is a part of life.

Open and honest discussions are the way forward. Often our instinct is to say, "Oh darling, that's not your concern right now," or to laugh questions off when our child asks about a topic we consider a societal taboo, but it's widely agreed by child development experts and family therapists that this has a negative impact without us even realizing it. The cure to "oversharing" and burdening our children with adult concerns is not to shut them out altogether. As with my experience of asking my mom to move out of our home, my children had some *big* questions, and despite their age, the best thing to do was to answer them as honestly as I could without going into detail.

We often make the mistake of "withholding to protect" or sometimes outright lying to our kids because the truth feels too painful. For example, questions like "Why does Gran buy things for my cousins, but she never even remembers my birthday?" are confronting. How do you answer that while protecting your child when the truth stings so deeply? I'm not suggesting you blurt out, "Um, because she's an asshole who only cares about my brother, her golden boy, and his family while totally forgetting me and mine," even though that might be the truth. That would be badmouthing; it's not acting in our child's best interests and is probably more about pulling them onto our side and gaining validation for ourselves. In the long run, honest and open should still be kind. I would reply, "That feels pretty unfair, doesn't it? Grandma has a better relationship with Uncle Dan, which is sad, and it means she focuses more on his kids. It's not about anything you do or don't do, sweetheart, it's not right or fair, but we can't force Grandma to change and it means she's missing out on so many wonderful moments with you." It's honest and kind, but above all, it focuses on what your child needed to know and needed reassurance of in that moment.

Not creating an open space for discussion, or withholding, means that we shroud things in shame and stigma, and we create a space where we end up looking like we can't be trusted. I have had countless conversations with cycle breakers who have fallen into similar traps, so I know this is a very common situation.

A note on being age appropriate

We covered this when discussing badmouthing; however, I want to reiterate that levels of understanding are different for different age groups and, indeed, amongst individual children.

You will know what your child will be able to understand and what they will struggle with, and that matters. Keeping it honest, open and kind creates a foundation of trust that is hard to break.

Avoiding making it "taboo"

During the early stages of cutting contact with my mom, my children were often cautious in mentioning her. It was like they were instinctually aware that there was hurt surrounding this person. We'd be in the kitchen and someone would say, "My friend is going to the water park this weekend. Do you remember when we went for my birthday? Me, you and Daddy would go down the slide while your sister stayed with . . ." and then they would trail off, a heavy silence filling the gap, with glances at me and each other to gauge how we were all going to react. It got to the point that anytime there was a mention of her or a memory that involved her, there was a level of discomfort. My mom had become a taboo, a no-go topic, and thus anything that could potentially involve her was suddenly awkward and cast in shadow and, to a degree, shame.

It's a common theme to feel like all "positive" memories are tainted somehow. It's something I hear a lot from clients who have started to reflect on their childhood now that they have their own children, especially, though not limited to, those who thought they were "really close" to their parent and experienced enmeshment. Trauma therapist and inner critic expert Maggie Nick, who goes by "Maggie with Perspectacles" online, often refers to "putting on the perspectacles." When talking with her on my podcast *Unfollowing Mum*, she explained that "perspectacles" is her term for viewing things from a new perspective, often our children's perspective, so that we can meet them in a healthy way and support their needs. When we become parents, we start to view *everything* from a new perspective, but nothing more so than our own parents, their parenting and our childhood, even in the healthiest dynamics. When we grew up in toxic dynamics, we take off the perspectacles given to us by those parents and replace them with new ones where suddenly we see those memories in a very different light.

It was no surprise that the kids were pausing and considering whether or not it was appropriate to mention my mom; after all, there was a lot of hurt and it was a big fracture in the family. What I did find surprising was how much their behavior brought up for me. I would lie awake and think, "Oh god, am I like her? Am I making them feel this way, like they are responsible for protecting my emotions and feelings?"

As with everything, open, honest communication saves the day. Whenever these moments would occur I would fill in the pause: "Maw Maw! Yes, I do remember my sister staying with her while we played, wasn't it the best?" Sometimes I would follow it up with, "Hey guys, I know it's tough because there has been this big fallout, but we can talk about her, OK? We all collected some great memories together—it's OK to still look back on them and enjoy them for the good times they were." Slowly but surely they began mentioning things again, and whenever there was a pause or a sense of uncertainty, I'd address it head on. One of the most important things in talking to children is to avoid creating stigma or making the topic taboo—in part we've been working toward that by being mindful not to badmouth and having open, honest communication, but an essential step is actively challenging any taboos that do crop up.

If you still have a relationship with your parent, albeit a difficult one, I would suggest welcoming questions such as the ones we saw in the badmouthing section. It's not uncommon for older siblings to position themselves as the "protector" of a parent, especially as they become more aware of the societal stigma around discussing toxic relationships (even if subconsciously). I once received a DM from a cycle breaker called Rosie (not their real name) asking for advice when their four-year-old had asked them, "Why doesn't your daddy ever hug you or say 'love you' when we leave, Mommy? Does he not love you?" Their older child, a teenager who was much more aware of Rosie's father's behavior, had jumped in and said, "Don't ask that! That's not kind."

To the younger child, it was a statement of fact, so you can imagine how baffling it would be at the age of four to be told that you were being unkind for asking a simple question. Rosie clarified that her father, who had raised her and her sister alone after their mother died when she was 11, was completely emotionally unavailable. They kept in touch, and she'd take the children over for Sunday dinner every so often, where he would criticize Rosie the whole time. When it came time to leave, he would just busy himself and say he'd see them later, leaving his wife to handle the goodbyes. There was no love there, he just didn't know how, Rosie told me, so as with most cycle breakers, she'd been determined to always make sure her children felt love and received lots of cuddles. In picking up on this, her youngest child had felt confused and wanted to ask about it— and it was *so* important that Rosie not only answered her question with honesty, but also addressed why it was OK to ask those questions and why her teenager wasn't responsible for protecting her. Shutting down is what creates stigma, and stigma leads to shame, which we discuss more on page 264 and is one of the most toxic things we can have in our lives.

What to do when your child starts asking about your childhood

It may be confronting as a cycle breaker when your child starts asking innocent questions about your childhood. You're presented with this little person who wants to find relatability where perhaps there is none, or wants to get to know what you were like as a child so they can feel closer to you. We all have a fascination with our roots; even as children we feel a curiosity about where we come from, and in turn where our parents come from. I distinctly remember sitting on my grandad's lap as a little girl and asking him to tell me about his childhood, what life was like for him. I also remember his face when I asked him one day what his experience of World War II was; a shadow passed over him, haunting him in ways I couldn't understand. As children we don't consider what the impact of our questions might be, we don't consider what our curiosity might bring up for the person we are asking—we ask away, uninhibited.

For many parents, sharing your childhood with your children is a beautiful experience—you gleefully show them your favorite places to visit, excitedly tell them about your firsts and watch their faces with anticipation when you introduce them to the movies that shaped your youth. Telling them tales of your childhood adventures (and misadventures) is a bonding experience filled with nostalgia and warmth. When you're a cycle breaker, that experience can be very different. What do you tell your children if the earliest memories you have are filled with violence and fear? It doesn't make for a fun bedtime story if your adventures consist of caring for a parent with addiction or staying out for as many hours as possible because home was a place where you couldn't be safe. How can you explain that you have some nice memories of your childhood, and on the surface it seemed OK, but actually it was filled with unhealthy behaviors and you spent most of your time unhappy? That so much of your time was spent walking on eggshells lest you receive weeks of silent treatment or be subjected to a vicious smear campaign that involved your parent telling everyone how dreadful you were and trying to encourage the rest of the family to "turn" against you? No, in those circumstances, these innocent questions can inspire deep anxiety and raise questions about what we can and can't be honest about.

So where is the line between honesty and oversharing? The last thing we want to do is trauma dump onto our children. This is how I navigate these questions—though let me assure you that, as with all things parenting, my children will sometimes blindside me with a question I don't know how to answer, or that triggers a memory I struggle to work through. Here are some tips on how to navigate those "tell me about your childhood" questions.

Vague honesty (at an age-appropriate level)

The same principle as we talked about on page 120 applies here: staying truthful but keeping it vague enough that it remains age appropriate. I appreciate sometimes it can be tough to know where the line of "age appropriate" is, as realistically this varies from child to child and depends on your own comfort level.

I remember my middle son asking me when he was eight or nine years old, "Mommy, why haven't we met your daddy?" To which I replied—honestly—"He died before you were born, darling. Remember, we talked about him dying when I was at college?" "Oh yeah," came the reply, followed swiftly by, "Why don't you ever mention him or have any pictures?" Darn. I thought I'd dodged this conversation. Suddenly the car was so silent you could hear a pin drop, as all three children waited in anticipation, sensing a juicy tidbit of information about my past. I smiled, my mind running at a hundred miles per hour trying to work out what I could say. I settled on the truth. "Well, darling, I didn't really see him very often as he wasn't a very good daddy to me. He left my mom when I was only four and unfortunately he chose not to make much effort to see me." Aha! I'd cracked it—vague and honest.

"Why did he leave?" came the curious reply. OUCH.

What could I say to this? I was definitely going to be bringing this conversation up with my therapist in our next session. My inner child wounds (see page 140) started stinging, all of those not-good-enough and abandonment feelings rippling underneath. I had a choice to make here: I could answer from that wounded child space, or I could answer from my adult space. Again, I thought back to what was vague but honest—what truth could I offer here that wasn't going to upset them or cause them to feel fearful? For many children, parents are on such a pedestal, they are infallible. To come to the realization that they aren't and can actively hurt their children, even if it's degrees removed, can be harsh and shocking. I have sat with clients whose children have heard stories of their childhoods and been overcome with emotions, or asked for reassurance in the form of, "But you'll never do that to me, right?"

I settled for, "I think that is a question that only he could really answer, my darling. When he met my stepmother, he decided he would rather be with her. Sometimes relationships don't work out—you have friends whose mommies and daddies live in separate houses, don't you? So that's what happened to me." Silence . . . followed by my eldest saying, "So he cheated? When he had a child? What a dick!" Great. Perhaps I should have leaned into the vague a bit harder . . .

I share this with you because this is the reality of these conversations. What ensued was a haphazard attempt to explain to my incensed son that, yes, what my father did wasn't a good thing, but people are flawed and make bad choices. It was incredibly confronting and uncomfortable to toe the line between wounded inner child and adult self who can see and appreciate the nuance of people's flawed behavior without excusing it, but it was important to try to facilitate the conversation rather than shutting it down.

When it's OK to say no

Sometimes we have experienced things in our childhood that we simply do not want to or cannot talk about, and that's OK. We are allowed to say to our children, "That's not something that I really like talking about. Maybe when I feel more able we can have a chat about this, OK? Thank you for asking though, shall we go do XYZ?" or, "Hmm, that's a big question! At the moment, I think maybe we need to wait to have that chat when you're older, OK? I didn't have a lot of the things you do when I was a child and it's a lot to understand. Thank you for asking though, shall we go do XYZ?"

Setting boundaries around what we're comfortable with is important—you're not shutting your children out or scolding them for asking questions, you're firmly and kindly outlining your comfort zone. One of the best ways in which we can encourage our children to set boundaries themselves is by leading by example and showing them exactly how to do it. It's also really important to teach them how to respect other people's boundaries, and again, these times are a perfect opportunity to model that behavior and give them the opportunity to see what it feels like when someone sets a boundary with you.

Journaling pages

- Write a letter to a friend, partner or family member who has let you down by "taking sides." You're not going to give them this letter, so include all your rawest feelings. Pouring your heart out onto the page and knowing that your words and feelings are safe as they won't go beyond the paper can be really healing. It's a way of achieving somatic release.

- Imagine an event from your childhood (or a feeling, if you struggle with childhood memories). Once you have a grasp on that scene/experience/feeling, I invite you to take a deep breath and imagine yourself, as you are now, going into that memory and talking to younger you in that memory. Telling younger you what they needed to hear in that moment, using empathy and kindness in the way you would speak to your child, allows you to offer yourself the validation that can be an integral part of healing.

Section 3

Parenting without a healthy blueprint

I'm sure you've started to realize that a lot of this "parenting" malarkey is actually about *you*, and not just how you relate to your child. So much of what we have been taught about parenting ignores this side of things, tells us to do this or that and it will all be just fine, but that isn't helpful for cycle breakers who are actively trying to unlearn a blueprint handed down through generations *and* repair the damage so often caused to them. I've often said we can't be the best parent we can be without knowing ourselves first. I certainly feel that when I first had my children, I didn't know myself well at all. In fact, I was oblivious, and I think my eldest child would be the first to tell you that I made some pretty whopping fails when it comes to breaking the cycle.

Over the next few chapters we are going to take a deeper dive into reparenting yourself, unlearning that unhealthy blueprint that comes with generational trauma, meeting your inner child on a deeper level and discovering your inner teen. We will also be looking at how we break the cycle in practical terms—helping your children to learn how to set boundaries (and how to cope with it when they set them with you!), navigating triggers, overcompensating and using different parenting styles. Finally, we will look at accountability and repair for when we *do* mess up.

Ready? Take a steadying breath and let's go.

Chapter 9

Reparenting you (while you parent)

As we have already discovered, a huge part of parenting and how we relate to our children is about us and what makes us tick as people. Our parenting journey starts way before we have children, with our own childhood and the ways we are taught parents and children interact, how we're taught to feel about ourselves, and the inner child we suppress. When the messages from our primary caregivers weren't healthy, we have to step up and reparent ourselves, which is what we're going to discuss in this chapter.

What does "reparenting" actually mean?

I hear this a lot—in fact, I distinctly remember one occasion on TikTok where I had been discussing reparenting and someone declared, "That is a made-up word! There is no such thing!" Well, all words are made-up words, and there is, in fact, such a thing as reparenting.

Reparenting is a term that refers to doing *inner child healing work*—essentially being your own parent, which you're probably doing often anyway (and if you experienced neglect, may have always done to some extent). We all have an inner child; we all carry them around with us every moment of every day, and they impact the way we think, react to others and navigate our lives. An inner child is that part of you that is childlike; it encompasses all the behaviors and personas you developed before puberty (after that is your inner teen, which we'll meet toward the end of this chapter). For some people, it's easy to think of an inner child in the more literal sense— as a little child living inside your mind, who holds all of those childhood memories, fears and feelings. For others it might be the connection you have to your younger self, and the memories from that time. However you choose to think of it, that inner child is going to be an important part of your life as a cycle breaker.

Why does inner child work matter from a cycle-breaking parenting perspective, you might ask? When we refuse to acknowledge our inner child, we allow them to go "unchecked," and along with them, the triggers we have accrued from our life experiences. An ignored inner child is like any other child craving but not receiving attention—they get loud, and they often take over. Think back to a situation where you reacted in a way that was emotionally immature. Don't worry, we've all done it. Maybe it was a disagreement with a partner, or a reaction to your child being too loud or not following simple instructions. I'd like you to think about how old you felt in that moment. This might take a bit of considering—you might be thinking, "I felt like myself, just frustrated and overwhelmed," and that's OK.

Often when we react to things in a way that is emotionally immature and, let's be honest, in a way that we would tell our children not to behave, it's because we're feeling our feelings from the place of a younger self. When I feel angry with my partner for not texting me to let me know where he is when he's running late, it's because I don't feel considered. My inner child immediately starts to feel neglected and abandoned, so I end up snapping at him or retreating when he comes home and feeling sulky. When my child won't listen to me, and is refusing to get to bed at the time I've set out, my inner child remembers how my parent would just leave me to go to bed whenever I wanted, often resulting in me being exhausted or gaming until late at night. The frustration, tiredness and overwhelm I feel at the end of the day bubbles up and takes over, while my inner child screams, "Don't they know how lucky they are!" Another common example for me happens at dinner times, when I've planned and spent time cooking my children a nutritionally balanced meal, only for them to declare, "*Ew*! I don't like it!" While adult me can look on and say, "That's frustrating, but that's kids. How can I make this situation work while also not becoming a walking cafe to five different palates?" my inner child is aghast. *All this effort and it's treated like nothing!* She remembers being constantly bullied for being overweight while being fed a steady diet of french fries, buttered pasta and fatty foods, or being allowed to choose mint chocolate chip ice cream for breakfast.

It's not just in those moments where you act out, but in the moments where your child reminds you of *you* that we face our biggest triggers. I recently experienced this with my daughter. It was coming up to her birthday and I'd got it in my mind that she'd probably aged out of birthday parties now.

Incorrect. Two weeks before her birthday, she started to talk about birthday parties, as if it was a given she was having one! I had to explain to her that this year wasn't going to be a birthday party year, but we could do something special over Easter or in the summer, which she was totally fine with. That night I clambered into bed and felt a sense of deep discontentment. I couldn't settle my mind at all. When I started to sift through my thoughts I kept coming back to the not-happening birthday party. My daughter said she was fine . . . but was she? I bet deep down she felt unloved, not considered, like I cared about her less than her brothers (who also hadn't had parties). I was absolutely messing this mom thing up. Sounds over the top and dramatic, right? Now what if you thought of those words coming from a nine-year-old girl? Still dramatic, but so are pre-teen children, navigating big emotions and reacting to things in a manner that we would consider "over the top" as adults.

When I was little, I remember one particular birthday party, where my mom hired the school hall, a DJ and really made a fuss over this *big* party and how much she had done for it. I felt so fancy, and what's more, my dad was going to come! The excitement was huge. I'm sure you can guess where this is headed—my dad didn't show up, or rather he did with only ten minutes left of the party, which my parents spent arguing. I spent the whole time before his arrival desperately upset while my mom raged about him and told me I was being ungrateful for not appreciating her efforts and enjoying myself.

In that moment, lying in bed and worrying myself over letting my daughter down over something that she really didn't seem that upset about, I wasn't considering these things from my adult self, but rather my inner child was feeding back to me all the ways in which they felt let down over birthday parties and how hurtful that experience had been *for me.*

Internal Family Systems theory (IFS)

IFS was founded by Richard C. Schwartz, who wrote the fantastic books *No Bad Parts, Introduction to Internal Family Systems* and *You Are the One You've Been Waiting For* to explain his theory and give us an insight into how we can develop some IFS practices at home. IFS philosophy works on the principle of multiplicity—we all have many parts. These parts are essentially *multiple inner beings* within us, with different ages, desires, opinions, talents and resources.

Under the IFS model, our "inner child" is actually an amalgamation of multiple "parts" of ourselves. I find breaking it down in this way to be a more holistic approach to healing. The "goal" of all our parts is the same—to keep us ticking, safe and happy. Your parts often get stuck at certain ages, each reflecting the way you felt at the stage it "developed." This might be a core memory, like being bullied at school and learning to feel shame for a physical feature; that "part" would forever be that age. Within IFS the goal is to have your "self" running the show. The "self" is viewed slightly differently by everyone—some prefer to think of it as the soul, others view it as the truest version of an individual—but regardless of what explanation you feel fits you best, your "self" will always be the real, adult version of you as you are now, who is ready to be responsible and caring for all the other parts. Just like a true parent would.

When I read about IFS philosophy, I found myself thinking of a meeting between my "self" (i.e. the parent/true version of me as I am now) and the other versions of me throughout time who had lost faith in me at some point, or perhaps never had a chance to meet me as my adult version, fully in control of this body we're all bumbling around in. During this imagining, I came to the realization that it is my job now, in my "self," to speak to these parts—the inner critic who tells me I'm not good enough, the part with crippling impostor syndrome, the fearful child who just wants to be "good," the child who feels abandoned and forgotten, the rage-fueled teen—and let them air their concerns, validating them and meeting them in a way that lets them know *I am the one they can trust now*. I find this approach really empowering, and I'd invite you to consider what inner parts you have.

IFS can be really useful in helping us understand those times when we have been doing—intentionally or not—the work on healing our inner child wounds, when we have started to set boundaries and make changes to our lives in a way that feels healthier and more authentic, and then suddenly we find ourselves experiencing anger. For a lot of people, anger is an emotion that they have fought to suppress, ignore or keep in check, so to suddenly find it present, to find themselves feeling irritable or even sullen, is a really strange sensation. I frequently experience this with clients who have either recently started to set boundaries with their parents, or cut contact, and feel that they have been making real progress only to suddenly feel rage toward their parents, the people who didn't help them when they were struggling as children. Some clients have described feeling petulant, argumentative and confrontational for no reason; whereas before they would always work to keep the peace, to be the good child, to fix, now they feel downright rebellious, and instead of keeping the peace, they want to disrupt it.

Perhaps this sounds familiar to you? Almost . . . teenage, would you say? We're going to talk a little more about the inner teen and navigating that experience on page 151. In IFS terms, an inner teen would be what we would consider a "protector part," who can be disruptive, angry, aggressive, apathetic and more. They step in front of that inner child part and "protect." These feelings of anger and irritation when you have made changes in your life and everything seems to be in a healthier, albeit reflective, place are so common and usually mask (or protect) those feelings of deep hurt that you're working through.

I'm not going to go too deeply into IFS theory—I have added some further reading to the Resources section should you wish to learn more—but I feel that it's worth noting this is yet another approach that centers *you* as the master of *your* little internal universe. Whether you view your inner child as a singular little being, or you choose to consider different versions of yourself, the truth remains the same: it's your responsibility to care for those inner yous and help them join you in the now.

How do I know if I have an inner child wound?

At this point I'm hoping we can agree that there is some kind of inner child (or perhaps many inner childlike parts of you) that is bumbling around as a part of your being, and frankly, they need some TLC and some understanding.

Let's take a look at the signs you might have a wounded inner child:

- You mask emotions and hold them in, often feeling discomfort around or avoidance of others' emotional displays too, especially if they remind you of your own child self.
- You feel like you have to please others, avoid rocking the boat and focus on "keeping the peace," even though it means sacrificing part of yourself.
- You avoid conflicts—especially with those you are close to. You may often feel resentful toward partners or family members because they haven't met your needs, but you probably haven't communicated them to avoid rocking the boat.
- Your feelings of self-worth are heavily linked to productivity or success, and you struggle with failings.
- You struggle to set boundaries and feel deeply guilty if you do.
- You don't receive criticism well, even if it's constructive.

If you're reading that thinking, "*Wow*, that sounds just like me," then don't worry, you're not alone. Earlier on we talked about how a lot of toxic parenting behaviors we endured as children were held up as the pinnacle of parenting. Children who were parentified or acted as "mini adults" were considered products of exemplary parenting. The reality is that our parents were creating inner child wounds, sometimes unintentionally and sometimes without care. We also live in a society that still struggles to accept the concept of inner child healing and views activities or hobbies that would facilitate connecting with your youthful side as inappropriate or wasteful uses of time. How many of us grew up with parents who would dismiss or deride our hobbies or passions instead of seeing them as viable career options? Or who demanded endless productivity rather than viewing our downtime as something precious, a time to recharge and learn to relax? It's no wonder we're all still carrying around these wounds and struggling to meet our inner child or childlike parts, when we've been conditioned to view them as nothing more than irritations (which may well align with the way you were viewed as a child by your parents and other adults in your life).

The four types of inner child wound

There are four main types of inner child wound that are helpful to understand (and yes, you can relate to all of them or more firmly with one!). In understanding them, we can learn how to avoid continuing the pattern of creating them. Take a look at the wounds listed below and see what resonates with you. It's OK if they *all* do—that's really common for people who have had toxic upbringings. And if some of the attributes seem negative or confronting, remind yourself that that is OK. In chapter 15 we talk about shadow work and accepting the sides of yourself that you perceive to be less than, but if you do find yourself feeling confronted by these inner child wounds and the way you react to people, then sit with that feeling and get curious. What messages have you been given about these behaviors or feelings you perceive as bad? Can you allow yourself to see why they are present for you, and if so, can you lean into those feelings and offer yourself kind words of encouragement that it's going to be OK, just like you would a child?

Getting to know what type of inner child wound you identify with is known as "wound mapping."

Abandonment wound

When we think of abandonment, we often think of separated parents, the death of a parent or some other kind of physical removal of a parent. But abandonment wounds show up because of emotional abandonment too. If you experienced a parent who was distant, closed off and/or rarely let you feel love, then the chances are you will relate to this one.

Abandonment wounds often show up as feeling "left out" or ignored in groups, even if you're present. You fear being excluded and will often try to "fit in" through a chameleon-like personality that suits whoever you're with. If you weren't invited to something, you would feel deeply hurt, and you can sometimes be overbearing as a friend or push people away before they get a chance to hurt you. This person will have found themselves attracting emotionally unavailable partners who are distant or mirror the behavior of their parent, and are prone to trying to convince others of their worth instead of just leaving toxic situations. You most likely hate being alone, or perhaps you feel lost when you're alone, as if you're struggling to work out who or what you should be. Your relationships will likely have been codependent, meaning that your sense of self and emotional wellbeing are reliant on others. When you're upset or feel hurt in a relationship, you often catastrophize or make threats to leave because to you that is the worst possible outcome, and if you get in there first, you're not being left.

Guilt wound

We talked on page 81 about FOG (fear, obligation and guilt), which is used by narcissistic parents to manipulate us into certain behaviors. People who have grown up experiencing this often present with an inner child guilt wound. While we refer to this type of wound as a guilt wound, it's not truly guilt that we are feeling, but rather shame that has taught us to believe we need to be guilty for everything and anything.

Guilt wounds are the things that make you feel bad for . . . well, everything! You may well find that you feel bad or guilty when setting boundaries, relaxing, saying no, or simply making a mistake that other people might just view as a mistake. You don't set boundaries in your relationships, or with yourself, and you likely find it really tricky when people— especially your children—try to set them with you. Need help? You won't ask for it, or if you do, it takes a monumental amount of effort. It's often noted in close relationships that you push away when you feel vulnerable and use the phrase "I'm fine!" even when you're really not. You might find that you ignore your own needs, because you fear being a burden or perceived as "needy," and you may experience others needing from you as confronting. Guilt wounds often lead to us using guilt-tripping to manipulate, even with the best intentions, because those are the patterns we have been taught. Guilt becomes a weapon to protect and get our needs met, while being the biggest cross to bear, instead of being a genuine feeling from our conscience.

Trust wound

Trust wounds are difficult to navigate; they're about losing trust not just in others but also in yourself, which is where the biggest challenges lie.

You likely find yourself fearful of being hurt, to the point that it holds you back in relationships or you find yourself with few close friends. You're unable to place your trust in others or your own decisions. It's healthy to consider others' opinions and thoughts; however, when we can't trust in ourselves, we begin to defer to everyone else and become prime targets for manipulation, or we become frozen in place waiting for others to tell us how to proceed. You feel insecure and often find validation through external sources, but rarely from yourself. If you achieve something, you will diminish it or not acknowledge it at all until someone else congratulates you (and sometimes even then you're uncomfortable, waiting for the punchline!). You rarely feel "safe" or "comfortable" with yourself or others—it's like there is always the expectation that something is about to go wrong or cause you harm, even if you're not actively aware of it. Your usual pattern of romantic relationships will be with someone unsafe, who withholds that validation you crave and feeds into the negative mindset that keeps you feeling like you're always about to be betrayed or hurt.

Neglect wound

As with abandonment, our minds often see the word "neglect" and jump straight to physical neglect or the worst-case scenario; however, physical neglect is not the only kind that can leave a mark. Emotional neglect is often even more impactful in creating this type of inner child wound because emotionally neglected children are consistently gaslit and have their feelings minimized by their parents, society and even themselves. Remember, there is never a competition in abuse—*all* abuse (which neglect is) is horrendous and undeserved. Abandonment and neglect wounds often team up, and you might notice a similarity in some of the signs.

With a neglect wound, you will often experience low self-worth, those feelings tied up in things like overachieving and perfectionism. You struggle to "let go" of things, often sticking around in relationships where you're underappreciated or treated poorly, trying to prove to the other party that you are worthy of their love, while believing you don't deserve better. You might stay in a toxic work environment or continue to accept that coffee with the friend who makes you feel inferior, because your inherent belief is that you are. You struggle with setting boundaries too, and as with a guilt wound, you struggle with others saying "no" and often feel rejected when it happens. Your fear of vulnerability means you rarely show when you're hurt, but unlike with the abandonment wound, you won't push away; instead you'll pull in and hold on tighter, pretending to be OK.

How do you feel about these types of wounds? Do any of them resonate with you in particular? Perhaps you have elements of all of them?

Self-awareness is key to unlearning patterns of behavior and healing. If you identify with any of these behaviors (or all of them), the next time you see yourself acting through this inner child wound, you can step forward as your adult self and have a "self-chat." This might look like you saying to yourself, "Oh, I know what is happening here—this is my inner child, and we're feeling rejected by my child asking for Daddy to read him a bedtime story instead of me. I want you to know, inner child, that it's OK. As much as it has stung us because we have that neglect and abandonment wound, I want my child to have a positive relationship with both parents, and I can read a story another night. It doesn't mean that I've done something wrong, or I'm a bad parent. We're all good. You can relax now." You can do this as a conversation out loud in the mirror, just talking to yourself while you make a cup of tea, or even in your imagination. I'd invite you to deepen your breathing as you have this self-chat: in through the nose for the count of four and out for the count of seven.

The biggest battles in inner child work are in self-acceptance and awareness. If you can manage these self-chats with compassion and kindness, I promise you these wounds will start to heal as your inner child flourishes under your care.

Cycle breaker's toolkit:
Exercises for connecting to
your inner child

Here are some ways in which you can help yourself feel more connected to your inner child. They might not all feel natural or comfortable for you, and that's OK. There's no need to force it, but I would invite you to gently revisit the ones you do find difficult, especially if you are struggling to feel compassion or love for your child self. This can build gently over time. There is a misconception that inner child work is really easy or natural, but it isn't for everyone. It's OK if you find it tough, but keep going. Remember, you're the adult now, and in the same way your children are deserving of love and kindness, so was your younger self, *and* so are you in the present.

1. Think of a positive memory you hold from childhood—I appreciate that this might seem a tricky ask if you don't have many positive memories, or memories at all, from growing up. If this feels like a struggle, don't force it. If you can capture a time you felt joy as a child, whether that was at school, at home, with friends or wherever, I'd like you to hold that memory in your mind and concentrate on what that child self was doing and how they felt. Did they laugh loudly? Maybe they had escaped to a storybook land or could feel a pet's fur on their hands? Who were they with? Allow yourself to feel their joy and feel so full of love for that child, as if they were your own.

2. Do you remember an activity you used to enjoy doing as a child? This might be Lego, art, imaginative play, reading, playing sports or something else. Reconnecting with those activities you used to love can be a great way to connect with your inner child. Indulging your childlike side isn't wasting time or being unproductive—it can be healing. If you're able, you might find doing this with your own child is helpful (or you may prefer to do it solo, and that's OK too).

3. Visualize yourself as a child—ideally around four to seven years old. If you have a photograph, go ahead and take hold of that to help you, if you feel able. Don't worry if this isn't sitting right for you—you can also visualize a representation of yourself at that age if it's too hard to think of yourself. This might be a teddy or a favorite toy, a little light burning brightly that represents you or something else. Now let's get talkative—you can do this via journaling, speaking or simply in your mind, whatever feels right. Just as if you were talking to anyone, it's time to ask your inner child some questions. What makes them smile? What makes them sad? What were they praised or punished for? What would they like to say to your parent if they could say anything? Who do they feel safe with, and what about that person makes them feel safe? When they feel sad, what do they do, who do they go to? What is their favorite color, game, TV program? You can ask as many questions as you like, but remember to listen and not force the answers. This is about getting to know your inner child and feeling

compassion for it, as if it was any other child you might chat with (perhaps your own!).

4. Find a quiet space where you can sit with your inner child, however you choose to visualize them. Step into the role of parent to that inner child. Let them know that you are there for them, you see them, you're going to be providing the love, comfort and protection for them from now on. There's no need for them to hide away or hold on to that shame. You've got it. I found this exercise—often called "reparenting practice"—brought up a lot of feelings for me. I was taken aback by my inner child opening up to me and I had an over-whelming urge to imagine them telling me their fears and sharing their hurt. I really struggled with inner child work and this felt like somewhat of a breakthrough moment for me. I had to wrestle with staying present and not dismissing myself as silly or "weird" for feeling the discomfort, but it truly impacted me on a deep level of connectedness.

5. Daily meditation is something you might not have expected to see here; perhaps you're like me and it conjures images of someone sitting on a yoga mat, connected to nature and relaxed. They don't have children running about and have all the time in the world to focus on breathing while they hum to maintain a perfect balance in their inner world. There is nothing wrong with this person, I just can't relate as a busy mom of three who can't go to the bathroom without someone asking a question or needing me to fix a squabble, so I certainly won't be able to meditate . . .

except I can and do. I picked up this particular practice of daily meditation from IFS (which we discussed earlier in the book), and I spend no more than 10–15 minutes a day, either in the morning or the evening when I'm in the shower. You could also try it on your commute. This can be a really helpful practice for people who struggle to think of an inner child as a small child just rumbling around in there, and who prefer to break this concept down further and think of their inner child as an assembly of multiple parts that stem from memories and events in their life. Take some deep, grounding breaths and focus the mind on meeting different parts of yourself, having a chat with them and finding out how they are feeling on that day. At first it feels silly—no point denying it—but after a while it becomes normal to say, "Oh hey, anxiety, you're feeling especially rowdy today, what's up? Ah, that event we're going to is freaking you out, huh? Hmm, I wonder where that stems from? Can we pinpoint a time this started? I want you to know that I'm here, I've got us and we're safe, OK? I'm the parent now." If you prefer, you can do this as daily journaling instead of meditation, but the pattern and purpose are the same—you're becoming more aware of who you are and what makes you tick, while reminding yourself you're in control of this ship.

Quick tip

Self-chats are a really powerful way to connect to your inner self and I'd actively encourage you to do them often, especially in front of your children. Encourage your kids to have them too—I do this regularly with my son who plays soccer; when I see him getting frustrated on the field, or overhear him doing his homework, he will quite often say things like, "C'mon, bud, we've got this."

Be mindful to encourage and lead by example with positive self-chats—if I hear him self-scolding, I will jump in and say, "Hey, be kind to yourself!" And he will often reply, "Er, yeah, you do it then!"

Nothing humbles you like your kids!

Let's meet your inner teen . . .

In the way that your inner child is a representation of your core needs and emotions developed in childhood, your inner teenager is responsible for *acting* on those needs and emotions, just as an actual teenager would.

When I talk to people about inner teen work, I'm curious about how they viewed themselves as an "actual" teen, and what messages they were given about themselves. My mom would tell me I was an "easy teen"—the problems started when I was in my twenties (i.e. when I became an adult with a wider frame of reference, and began developing a sense of self). But actually, I was a struggling teen. I had around 22 percent attendance in my last few years at school because I often just didn't want to go and had no adult who would step in and set boundaries to make me. On one occasion I remember feeling so fed up with my life that I raided the drinks cupboard after Mom had gone to work, unable to put into words that it "soothed" my nerves and anger, to take the edge off. At 15 I thought it would be a good idea to head into school and enjoy science after a few whiskeys. No one noticed. On more than one occasion as a teen and young adult, from age 13 to 22, I got so drunk after spending time with friends that I couldn't stop vomiting and eventually passed out—all facilitated by my "cool" mom, who would let me have parties at home with big boxes of mixed alcohol beverages we'd bought together from the wholesaler, but who would then shame me for getting drunk and being a "binge drinker." My experiences with heartbreaking crushes and toxic men started early, but unlike those of a normal adolescent, my crushes would be less about teasing or ignoring and would come laced with shame or sexual warnings about who I was and what my sexuality would mean. I would be told I was "loose" and had "always been interested in men, even as a baby" so needed to behave myself because "sluts sleep around." As long as I didn't do that, I was OK; meanwhile any idea of investigating my sexuality would be slapped down with an "I'm all for the gays, just not my child" attitude and reminders of how much I loved men so not to be silly and indulge this curiosity.

Given the constant sexualization that I experienced growing up, it's no surprise that at 15 I met a man ten years my senior, who groomed me over a three-year relationship that culminated in him leaving me for another woman only seven months after we got married when I was 18. At the time that was devastating, but now I can see it as a very lucky escape. I was polite, kind and easy to be around. Like all adolescents, I was quite content to snooze the day away given the chance, and I hated chores, but I had my sights set on being an adult and owning my own business so I could be in charge of myself and free. I was often described as an old head on young shoulders, but reading this story back, I feel I was far from it—it was just more convenient for people to accept that mask I put on, rather than see the reality.

I wasn't an "easy" teen, I was failed. I was desperately trying to find love that was consistent and reliable, but had none of the tools to realize that *love needs to be primarily found from within.*

You might read this and relate to my experience, or perhaps yours was the opposite. Maybe you were told you were a nightmare teen, but actually you were the stable member of the household, caring for siblings and dealing with things way beyond your scope. Maybe you were rebellious and moody with authoritarian parents; perhaps you fell in with the "wrong crowd" because any crowd was better than being bullied or being alone at home. There are a million and one ways that your teen years could have gone, but usually with a dysfunctional family, the messages we were given about ourselves as teens are wholly different from the experience we actually lived.

If you haven't done so yet, I invite you to take a moment and think about the messages you have been given about yourself as a teenager—these might be from parents, siblings, extended family, friends or other adults in your life at the time. Once you have a clear idea of how you were portrayed, I'd like you to think about how you *actually were.*

You might find it helpful to jot these thoughts down on a piece of paper. I encourage you to think critically about those messages you were given if they were negative and your perception is also negative. Were you really "difficult," or were you striving for autonomy, struggling or perhaps just experimenting? What constituted "difficult" or "easy" to your parents or the people around you? What did it mean for you? If you find yourself thinking about your teen years in an especially negative way, get curious as to why.

Now we've talked about you as a teen, but what about your *inner teen*? Similar to an inner child, our inner teen is a part of us that holds our memories, beliefs and emotions from a certain period in our lives, viewing things through that lens. For the inner teen, it's our adolescent years and mindset. Wounded inner teens tend to hold a lot of anger, shame and frustration in addition to the rebellion and independence that is a part of all healthy inner teens. Have you ever thought, "You can't tell me what to do?" and then upon reflection felt you were being a bit immature (even if you'd never admit it?). Say hi to that inner teen driving the vehicle on this one.

When clients tell me that they have been working on their inner child, soothing the fears and sadness that they have experienced at the reality of their relationship with their parent, they often describe reaching a point where they feel deep anger, especially if they still have contact. More often than not they feel obstinate and irritable about even the slightest things, similar to how they did as a teen. I remember working with one client who described to me feeling a bit like a grumpy teenager during interactions with her parents, who she had been successfully limiting contact with in a bid to set some firmer boundaries and have some kind of relationship. She'd gone from feeling guilt and shame with every text message she received, to eye rolling and feeling a complex mix of anger and a desire to push back, even when it wasn't needed. My client didn't want to cut contact completely, and her parents had a positive relationship with her children despite the fractured one they had with her. But she felt that in some ways her own behavior had transformed; she'd gone from always being the mature one in the relationship with her parents, often parenting her mom, to reliving the teen years she never allowed herself to have.

When we break this down it makes absolute sense that an adolescence denied resurfaces when it is safer to do so. If you can convince your inner teen that you are a safe, responsible adult now, who is going to take charge and reparent them through the previously mentioned work, then they are going to step aside (always with you, but no longer taking over) and allow other suppressed feelings, memories and emotions to come to the fore.

Another common experience I encounter when working with clients is the person who has a relationship with their parents but feels like they regress every time they are in their presence—sometimes to a small, vulnerable child who just wants to be loved and is jumping through hoops, but often to a grumpy, argumentative teen who picks fights and grumbles at everything. It's very important here to note that there is often an overlap with the "I must be the problem" narrative we are given by toxic parents—being told you're difficult, unpleasant to be around, always causing drama, etc.—and the way we perceive ourselves in our parents' presence. Much like the exercise above where you considered yourself as a teen and sorted what was fact from what was a narrative given to you, I invite you to do the same here. I'd also like to note that this might not be a way you *act*—perhaps outwardly you are the in-control adult, but internally you're filled with rage and hurt that you have to work to silence in your parent's home. If you come to the conclusion that you do find yourself slipping back into a past version of yourself, this might be because your inner teen is taking charge and your parents' behaviors and/or your relationship with them (historically or now) brings up something for you that you've not yet worked through.

What wounds our inner teen?

Rejection

Rejection is hard to cope with at any time, but especially during our teen years, when those rejections seem to come thick and fast, all while we're navigating hormones and new life experiences and stretching for autonomy. If you find that rejection at home, it compounds those wounds.

Bullying

For many people, bullying is something that takes place at school or in group settings with peers, but for children of toxic parents, bullying often happens at home too. Merely existing as a teen can be complicated enough, but having to walk on eggshells and survive a critical, abusive or violent parent is a whole other level. We grow up so quickly and there is a loss that comes back in the form of a wound.

Negative self-image

Something you will find in all children of toxic parents, whether those children go on to be internalizers (people-pleasers) or externalizers who follow the pattern of their parent's abusive behavior, is that a negative self-image is at the core. We develop so much of our "self" in our adolescence, and when you already have the negative bias that you are somehow horrible or unworthy, this wound is created.

Lack of control, especially during major changes

This could be due to a number of factors—ill health, death of a parent, changing schools, financial issues, etc. When we lack control over our lives, especially if we live with a toxic parent who expects us to be the scapegoat (the one to blame for any and all problems) or the fixer (responsible for fixing everyone's messes!), we end up ignoring our needs and creating wounds that continue to bleed.

Parentification

This is probably the deepest cause of inner teen wounds I see. To deny a child their childhood, and an adolescent their teenage years in which they can feel safe to make mistakes, act out and develop an identity, is to bind them, holding them *in situ* until they can feel safe to be free again. I see so many people and speak to thousands more every day who have experienced parentification (see page 38) and feel the impact of that wound deeply.

As with your inner child, there are some ways in which you can work with your inner teen. I want to caveat again that this work is *work*, and it's OK if you find it hard. Inner child and inner teen work takes time and is a constant process. As we come to the close of this chapter, remember that even with these exercises, you're not expected to have all the answers all at once. Sometimes, meeting your inner teen first can be helpful to pull back the veil on that younger and more vulnerable you. In the next chapter we're going to look at what kind of parent you want to be and build upon healing those wounds.

Cycle breaker's toolkit: Inner teen exercises

1. Remember the inner child exercise that encouraged you to do things you loved as a child? Well, part of connecting with that inner teen is having experiences that feel a bit wild. I'm not suggesting you get black-out drunk or try drugs—we're just dipping our toes into being a bit carefree, not launching ourselves backwards. Think about ways you can reconnect with those teen experiences that you may not have had, such as going to concerts, gaming, dressing in fun outfits, getting that tattoo or piercing you were told you shouldn't get, going out with friends and partying (responsibly . . . ish) and letting loose in the ways that you would have liked

to try. If you're feeling a lot of anger, rage rooms are a great outlet.

2. Core belief exercises can be powerful for inner teen healing. I'd like you to think about how you feel about yourself, other people and the world at large. Do you often make negative remarks about those things? Perhaps you find yourself saying things like, "I'm so horrible at organizing things!" if you make a reasonable mistake or forget to add something to your calendar. Maybe you view the world as a dark place, or you feel strongly that other people will always let you down. Jot down some of the core beliefs that you notice in yourself—this might be a process that takes a period of time, it doesn't have to happen all at once. Once we notice and become aware of our core beliefs, we can start to ask questions, challenge them and adjust according to evidence. You can hold these beliefs in your mind and every time you notice negative self-talk, pause, step back and challenge them with evidence.

3. Accepting and validating the inner teen is a huge part of healing work. We can start with affirmations and visual-izations, similar to the inner child exercises we discussed on page 147; however, when we're dealing with an inner teen we're going to imagine speaking to them with respect and kindness, and hear their fears. Affirmations might sound like, "You are good enough as you are," or, "You're safe and loved. You can be whoever you want to be." These will be personal to you—if you're struggling, search "empowering affirmations for teens" online for some ideas and adapt however you see fit.

Tip: Lean into the areas in which you were especially shamed. For example, if you were shamed for making mistakes, choose affirmations that let your inner teen know that you can and will make mistakes, and that's OK because you can be accountable if or when a mistake hurts yourself or others; mistakes can be mended and you can move on. How do you feel if you say aloud the words: "I trust you, I love you, I will still be here for you if you mess up"? If that elicits a strong response from you, that's an area of pushback from your inner teen, and I invite you to let them know until the message sinks in.

4. Explore *you*. Explore your style, likes, dislikes, the things that make getting up in the morning worth it, foods you enjoy, hobbies that make you smile.

Chapter 10

What kind of parent do you want to be?

We've talked about you as a child, you as a teen, your own parents and *their* parents . . . but what about you as a parent? If I were to ask you, "What kind of parent do you want to be?" you'd probably tell me that the only thing you know for sure is that you don't want to be like your own parents. Or perhaps you would say, "I just want to be a good one," but what does it mean to be a "good" parent?

The good (enough) parent

We all have different ideas of what makes a "good" parent, so much so that you will seldom find two people who agree on everything they think qualifies as "good." Someone might say, "Well, a good parent isn't abusive," but we then have to define what is and isn't abusive in our own minds, and that will look different for each of us. It's why parenting with your partner can be so tough, why you feel so judged by others at times—

be it a family member or a complete stranger. To one person, your gentle, soothing words during a child's temper tantrum over being told they can't have a lollipop, or your ability to keep your cool even though they are snot-bubbling their way through the pasta aisle at the grocery store, is "good" parenting. To others it's slack, lazy parenting and not disciplining the child will create further problems down the line. Before you know it, they are facing jail time because you let them get away with so much (who knew your reaction to a toddler tantrum over a lollipop would have such severe consequences?). Parenting is a very individual thing, built on a foundation of your experiences, your parents' parenting, societal and cultural norms, and so much more. The purpose of this book isn't to tell you how everyone should parent, but to empower you with the tools to parent *in your way* and create a strong, healthy relationship with your child that lasts beyond the "18 summers" social media tells us we have.

First things first, let's do some reframing. Let's think less about a "good" parent, and more about a "good enough" parent. Would it surprise you if I told you that in order to create a solid foundation with your child, you only need to be attuned to their needs 30 percent of the time? Let's sit with that for a second. How does that make you feel? I'd imagine it's a mixture of relief that you don't have to suddenly morph into an all-knowing, all-seeing oracle to be a good parent, but also some complicated feelings surrounding your own parents. That's OK. If you need to, pop the book down for a minute and take some time to do something else—have a mindless scroll online, get out for a walk, do something fun with your kids. Come back when you're ready.

The 30 percent theory, which came from studies into

attachment theory conducted by Dr. Donald Winnicott in the 1950s, doesn't mean that we can completely mess it up the other 70 percent of the time, but rather that *we need to be* "attuned to our children's needs," wholly, for that 30 percent. If you're a parent now, how often have you known, instinctively, that your child needs food when they are screaming in their stroller, or that they are moody when they come home from school? I'm willing to bet that you have memories of other people turning to you and saying, "How do you know what they want just from that little grunt or movement?" And you would dismiss it and say, "Ah well, I'm with them all the time!" Or, "It's my kid so I guess I just do!" That right there is you being attuned. When we're not so sure, especially as they grow into adolescence, we can ask questions, create a safe space for them to talk to us if they need to and work on our own self-awareness to challenge our prejudices and biased ideas.

There are hundreds of different "types" of parenting, with new terms popping up on social media all the time—crunchy parents, gentle parents, free-range parents, helicopter parents, authoritarian parents and more. However, most of these categories fall into four main types of parenting. These are **authoritarian, authoritative, permissive** and **neglectful/ uninvolved**.

Let's have a look at these in a bit more detail. Take a look at the image on the next page. Hopefully what it shows is that while no parenting style is perfect, we're aiming to be in that highly responsive but also more demanding bracket: the authoritative parent. In this context, high demand doesn't mean having unrealistic, unattainable expectations, but simply *having* expectations and aspirations for your child and

High demand

Authoritative | ## Authoritarian

- has firm but flexible boundaries
- respects autonomy but also has rules
- rational control/structure
- responsible
- collaborative

- high expectation/ perfectionism
- no discussions, my way or the highway
- rigid
- scary/aggressive at times
- uses terms like "disappointed"
- controlling

High responsiveness ———————————→ **Low responsiveness**

- child led
- lacks boundaries
- overindulges to be the "friend" figure, sometimes emotional parentification
- respects autonomy but doesn't provide structure or rules
- no consequences to learn

- disengaged
- absent physically or emotionally
- doesn't praise or encourage
- instrumental parentification

Permissive | ## Uninvolved

Low demand

encouraging them to fulfill their potential in a way that benefits them, not you. Here we have boundaries, but we're collaborative; we have consideration for our child's autonomy and their need for self-discovery, but we facilitate that within a safe, structured environment, and we're willing to step back and view our own faults. I think it's really important to note, especially for cycle breakers who recognize their parents in one or more of the other types, but especially the authoritarian and permissive parents, that authoritative parents mix together the qualities of the other parenting types to find a balanced place in the middle.

My favorite way of thinking of this is as a pendulum—on one side you have authoritarian parents and on the opposite you have permissive. Your pendulum swings one way or another—too often when we have experienced authoritarian parents we try to swing *all* the way to permissive because we have suffered the impact of their demands for perfectionism, aggressive moods and controlling behavior. Every parent will likely have traits of certain parenting styles, usually because of the way in which we are raised, the cultural norms of our society and the current trends in parenting, but it's important to remember that we are seeking balance in our parenting. It's OK if your child is upset with you sometimes and it's OK if you have to "be the bad guy" and they have to face consequences for their actions at times. Equally, it's OK to hold your child if they are crying and allow them to share their emotions without trying to snap them out of it, and it's OK for them to have opinions and to collaborate on the rules you set in the house.

Many of us grew up hearing the words (or some variation of them), "This is my house and what I say goes," and while that's true to some extent—as the responsible adult it's your job to create and enforce rules—teaching our children that the place they live in isn't theirs is unhelpful and creates a sense of insecurity and a deep wound. By letting them know "this is *our* home, but I'm the responsible adult, so we have to have some rules—let's talk about them," we create a sense of collaboration within the safety net of being that responsible adult.

Let's look at some examples of these types of parenting. Remember, if you feel that you see yourself in some of these examples and it makes you uncomfortable, that is OK. It doesn't make you a bad parent. We are learning constantly. Get curious about why it's hit so close to home and how you can make changes that work for you.

Scenario	
Your preschooler bites another child at a playgroup because they want a toy. They take the toy and the other child is left crying.	
Permissive parenting	This parent might say, "Oh no, that wasn't kind," and instead of correcting the behavior, let the child continue playing with the toy so as not to upset them, but feel awkward and leave soon after. The intention is to avoid upsetting the child because this is normal developmental behavior, but they don't receive the behavior correction needed to avoid the situation again. They don't learn.
Authoritarian parenting	This parent might grab their child, hand the toy back to the other child and give theirs a "telling off," which could look like telling them what they have done is naughty/horrible, placing them in the naughty corner so they can't play for a period of time, or even smacking them. The intention is to stop this happening again, and to let the other parents and the child know that this behavior isn't tolerated. While the child might learn, they learn through fear and shame, which damages their relationship with the parent and themselves.
Neglectful parenting	This parent might shrug and say, "Kids will be kids," and go back to their phone or magazine, completely removing themselves from the situation, even though their child has hurt someone. There is very little intention here, more an ambivalence toward parenting and a self-centered attitude. The child not only doesn't learn, but they have no gentle prompts and are abandoned to work things out for themselves.
Authoritative parenting	This parent might step in and say, "Oh dear, that wasn't kind, can you say sorry? I know you really wanted the toy, but it wasn't OK to bite. Let's give that toy back and you can come and sit with me while we have a few minutes to calm down." They would hand the toy back to the other child and remove the child from the situation, but stay with them to regulate together. The intention is to correct the behavior *and* help the child understand what went wrong, while enforcing the consequence of sitting out but remaining present. In working through this together, the child can develop social skills and boundaries, but do so without fear or shame and knowing that their parent is a safe space.

Scenario	Your young child is crying every day at the school drop-off and struggling with separation anxiety. The school tells you they are fine when they are settled into class within a few minutes of you leaving and this is all very normal, it's only been a few weeks. Your child tells you they like school, they just don't like it when you go.
Permissive parenting	This parent might allow their child to miss school instead of sending them in because they feel too guilty or worried themselves. They might insist on walking the child to class or even pull their child out of school altogether, without giving them time to adjust in a safe and secure manner.
	The intention is to avoid the child feeling abandoned and potentially (subconsciously) soothe anxieties for not just the child but the parent too. Not giving the child a chance to see that you will always return for them and that school is a necessary part of their development creates potential codependency.
Authoritarian parenting	This parent might respond by getting frustrated with their child and telling them to get a grip, using shaming language or harsh words to "toughen them up."
	The intention is to get the child to stop crying and clinging to the parent because these behaviors are often considered weak. Many authoritarian parents haven't had soothing or emotional regulation modeled to them, and seeing a child crying and in need can bring up feelings of being out of control (which is a fundamental part of authoritarian parenting). Eventually the child stops crying, but instead of learning to soothe their anxiety, they bottle it up and it presents in other ways.
Neglectful parenting	This parent might show they are annoyed by the crying because they want to get on with their day. They offer no reassurance; instead they likely reinforce the fear of abandonment by turning up late or not showing up to meetings/important events.
	The intention isn't focused on the child's needs but the parent's. They might need or want to get to work or have something else they feel is more important than the child's needs. While most parents have to draw a line because of commitments, they would explain this to the child and try to find a resolution—a neglectful parent won't consider the child's needs at all. The child learns they aren't important or valued.
Authoritative parenting	This parent might explain to their child that they know this is tough but offer them reassurances, using a calm voice, ultimately leaving them and letting them know exactly when they can expect them to return.
	The intention is to soothe the child while also maintaining the boundary that school has to be attended. This parent places their child's needs at the fore, even though they may feel a combination of all the other emotions the other parents do. They choose to encourage, not shame, and follow through on promises.

Scenario	
Your tween (9–12) child has been in trouble at school for disruptive behavior, falling out with peers and not doing homework.	
Permissive parenting	This parent might react in defense of their child. They struggle to see the child is at fault, and if they are able to see it, they choose not to act because that may upset the friendship-like connection they have with their child. There are no consequences for their child's actions.
	The intention is to protect the friendship-like relationship that supersedes the responsible parenting needed. Often inadvertently this parent becomes an enabler. The child may feel happy in the moment, but they lack boundaries and are often left feeling insecure or without guidance.
Authoritarian parenting	This parent might react with harsh punishment, shouting or even physical punishment. They are unlikely to listen to their child's side of the story, instead reacting in condemnation of their child. Shaming language like "I'm disappointed in you" is very common.
	The intention here is to raise a "well-behaved" child, but the result is often the opposite. By not hearing their child out and always "siding" with other people without fact-gathering first, they create a rift in the relationship and their child struggles with self-esteem.
Neglectful parenting	This parent might ignore the school's contact, or respond with, "Well, that's something for you to deal with" to the child or the school (or both). They essentially remove themselves from the situation.
	The intention is to avoid accountability and not spend time on the situation. They aren't defensive or condemning, but just expect to not be involved as it's between school and the child. This can often lead to an increase in "bad" behavior as the child seeks support and attention in other ways to get their needs met.
Authoritative parenting	This parent might hear out the school and then ask their child for their version of events. If needed, they will issue consequences to correct the behavior, steering clear of shaming language but explaining—even if their child thinks it's unfair or is upset/angry with them—that actions have consequences and it's their responsibility to help guide their child to make better choices.
	The intention here is to be reasonable and hear the child out. Asking *why* this has happened is a fundamental difference from other parenting styles—here the parent wants to understand and then work with their child and school to fix things. They aren't afraid to upset their child and have consequences, but they also won't be overly critical or harsh. The child, while potentially upset at the consequences, learns boundaries and has stability.

Scenario
Your teenager has been lying to you about going to parties and drinking, and they have now been caught vaping and selling vapes at school.

Permissive parenting	This parent might say things like, "Teenagers are meant to experiment," or, "I keep telling them, but I just can't do anything to stop them!" They don't set firm boundaries or enforce consequences for the behavior.
	The intention is to avoid upsetting their child or being the "bad guy" and also to avoid accountability for their child's behavior and lack of boundaries. The child continues to lack structure and boundaries and doesn't experience consequences.
Authoritarian parenting	This parent might react with rage or aggression; they may take away the child's most prized possessions or enforce harsh punishments in order to create consequences, without giving much thought to impact. They will often use shaming language.
	The intention is to enforce consequences for their child's actions, but they are also trying to avoid accountability for their child's behavior by not considering the "why" behind this event. The child will either hide future activities or become more rebellious and learn that conflict is handled with shame and aggression.
Neglectful parenting	This parent, much like in the previous scenarios, may pass the responsibility back to the child or school with phrases like, "Well, what do you want me to do about it?" or be unreachable and refuse to be involved.
	There is little interest or intention with a neglectful parent other than to avoid involvement. The child learns they don't matter to their primary caregiver and feels abandoned, angry and fearful.
Authoritative parenting	This parent might react with appropriate consequences after considering the "why" behind the event. They will likely discuss it with their child and school, consider what has led to this situation and look outward for support if needed.
	The intention here is to focus on helping the child, understanding why this has happened and what can be done to support them. They will issue age-appropriate consequences for their actions, but the intention is to teach them that there are consequences to actions, not to shame or punish them through hurt or fear.

You might read through these examples and think, "Right, well it just sounds like you're describing the 'perfect' parent with the authoritative parent—we can't behave like that all the time. How unrealistic!" and you'd be absolutely right. These examples are just that—examples of each type of parenting in the truest form to give you an idea of what style you might recognize from your childhood and what you identify with the most. In reality, we're a blend of these parenting types, with one at the core (the goal being a healthy blend and balance—which is what authoritative parenting is). For example, if you look back at the image on page 164, you might consider yourself a mostly authoritative parent, but you're sitting really close to the line with permissive and sometimes you jump over. It's a spectrum, and one that we will forever be developing and evolving.

In some parenting books, you won't see neglectful parenting acknowledged, but instead you'll see an image reflecting three types of parenting, like the one below. What we see in this image is the way authoritative parenting blends permissive and authoritarian styles to find a healthier middle ground. The reason I didn't lead with this image is because I think it's important for cycle breakers to see their childhood experiences acknowledged and understand *why* they need to be aware of breaking that cycle, validating their inner child and not falling into the pendulum trap where they swing from one side (their parent's parenting) to the extreme opposite. We could expand on the image on page 164 to include neglectful on one side, the extreme of permissive, and bullying on the other side, the extreme of authoritarian.

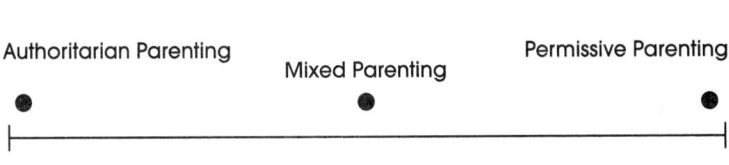

AUTHORITARIAN-PERMISSIVE PARENTING CONTINUUM

All parents will shout, lose their tempers, sometimes let their kids stretch their boundaries, occasionally avoid putting boundaries in place because they don't want the hassle (until that bites them on the ass and they have double the work to do) and even ignore their child's needs because they just want five minutes' peace. We all do it. Balance is the key.

What to do when you recognize you're not finding balance

As we have already discussed, balance isn't about getting it right all the time (remember that 30 percent stat from earlier!), but sometimes we recognize that we have been falling into the pattern of being overly permissive, too harsh with our children or simply not considering their needs. As cycle breakers, these realizations are going to hit us hard. We want to be the best parent we can be for our children, and we want them never to experience the things we did growing up— whether we have repaired the relationship with our parents in adulthood or not. It makes perfect sense that we would not only find it really confronting to realize we are getting it wrong, but also that we are more predisposed to struggle with balance because we're battling against repeating cycles and trying *so* hard not to be our parents.

We will all lose the balance sometimes, but when you notice that this is happening for you, take a step back from yourself, take some deep breaths and consider the following:

- How do I want to parent here and how am I parenting?
- What does my child *need*, not want? Do they need me to be the "bad guy" and enforce some boundaries? Do they need me to back off and respect their autonomy a bit more?
- What do *I* need? Am I struggling with my own mental health or burnout from all of the daily stresses?
- What result am I looking for here? Is it to get my kid to school? Maybe it's to have them clean their bedroom without me having to lose my temper?
- How can we collaborate to get to that result? I could set boundaries around going to school but also find out what is causing them to not want to be there. I could liaise with teachers and work out a plan that supports them. I could set a timer and clean their room with them as much as we can in 15 minutes, then have a break and come back for another 15 minutes later.

It's OK if you sit with these questions *after* there has been a rupture in your relationship with your child. Perhaps you have yelled and lost your temper over the untidy room and you need to adjust your expectations (this is me!), or you've forgotten something important to them at school and feel really guilty. Or maybe you've not been setting boundaries and now you're struggling to get them to do the things that they have to do. We talk about accountability and repair in greater detail in chapter 14, but remember that being able to admit when you've made a mistake, set boundaries and have those uncomfortable conversations is part of being a cycle breaker—not aiming for a perfection that doesn't exist.

Chapter 11

Triggers and how to deal with them

I remember once being told that your children will trigger you in ways that you never knew possible, and it's one of the truest things I've ever heard. "Triggers" are a hot topic on social media, with the word often being weaponized and used as an insult. You might see comment sections filled with lines like "omg she's so triggered" and "stop being so triggered," or people declaring "this has triggered me," but what does it actually mean?

The *Oxford English Dictionary* defines "triggers" as "a response to a particular action, process or situation." To go a little deeper, when we talk about someone being "triggered" in psychology, it's something that sets off a *deep emotional and/or physical response to a memory* we hold either within our minds or on a cellular level. This is usually something that you wouldn't expect to cause a reaction—perhaps it's the smell of a certain perfume or the taste of a certain alcohol. It could be an innocent noise or a visual on a screen, but it's personal to you and is likely to "trigger" a memory that will cause a visceral reaction. Triggers are usually the

reason we lose our temper, become frustrated or find ourselves needing to step away, and they are a source of shame,
guilt and confusion for many.

No one and nothing is ever quite so triggering as our
children. Watching them live out experiences can bring up a
flood of things for you—even if their experience isn't negative,
or anything like yours, it only has to recall a memory for your
sympathetic nervous system to jump into action. This is especially prevalent as they reach ages of specific events in your
life—positive or negative, but usually negative—because you
will see so much of yourself in them. These things can take us
by surprise and leave us feeling ashamed or silly, but I can
promise you that you're far from alone when it comes to
experiencing triggers from your children. Let me share with
you a few of the ways in which I've found myself triggered and
been launched back to a memory or feeling with my own
children.

Remember my story about my daughter and her birthday
on page 135? She didn't want a birthday party, until she
changed her mind about ten days before her birthday.
Suddenly she wanted a big party, a sleepover with Harry
Potter bedding and tents and snacks and "Oooh, Mommy, we
could give everyone pajamas!" Needless to say, the big
sleepover was out, but I looked into booking the trampoline
park she suggested. After a bit of deliberation, we agreed that
it was a no this year—we'd not long come back from a big
vacation, the boys hadn't had parties and did we *really* need
to spend hundreds on a party now? I suggested a party at
home in the summer, maybe a sleepover too, when I'd had a
bit of time to plan and prepare (mentally and physically,
because I am *not* a party mom!). My daughter was a bit

disappointed, but ultimately fine with it—she shrugged and started to get excited about having a Taylor Swift party in the summer. Despite her reaction, I had a really uneasy feeling. I felt like I'd ruined some fundamental part of her childhood, and in years to come she would remember this as the moment we stopped caring about her birthday and started to do less and less.

After a bit of deliberation, I worked out what was bothering me and, surprise surprise, it really had nothing to do with the little girl upstairs in her bedroom belting out "Cruel Summer" on full blast. It did, however, have everything to do with the little girl *in me*, who she reminded me so much of. Birthdays are a sensitive area for me, as they are for a lot of adult children raised by narcissistic parents. One of my core memories of birthdays as a child is my mom renting part of the middle school opposite our house to have a roller disco party for me (at least I think there were roller skates, although it may well have just been me in them!). I think I would have been around five to eight years old. I was so excited. This party was a *big* deal. My mom made such a fuss about how much work she had put in, how she'd hired a DJ and how much it had all cost! Oh, the cost, especially for a single parent whose deadbeat ex wasn't contributing! Speaking of my dad, he had promised to come along to this party, and as my parents were warring their way through the divorce courts, I didn't see him terribly often, so I was beyond excited (something that bothered my mom no end). I remember very little of a lot of my childhood between the ages of 4 and 11, but I remember the *feeling* of excitement. I remember falling out with friends and sitting in a corner crying because my dad didn't turn up until 15 minutes before the end, and I remember the argument when he did eventually turn up outside in the dark, and my mom's friends ushering me in, away from my parents. There were so many big feelings around this event for little me—deep abandonment, shame, sadness and fear. My mother was livid my dad had spoiled the party for me, but also livid with me for not getting on with the evening and wasting all her time, money and effort (something she would absolutely deny when confronted in adulthood with a casual, "You remember things funny, you do!"). That was, as far as I recall, the last birthday party I had.

This isn't an especially bad story, and you might be thinking, "OK, sad for the kid, but come on, let it go, you're an adult now!" Our triggers don't necessarily make sense, and they don't always have to be tied to huge events, but they will be tied to things that mattered to *us* and changed how we viewed the world, even if only in a slight way. My inner child remembers how it felt to be disappointed over a birthday party, and so she took the reins, reminding me of those feelings and warning me that I needed to be so careful not to make my daughter feel that way—but also highlighting that this wound was still hanging around.

Another all too common trigger is the first time your child starts school, or in my case when my eldest child started being bullied because he was a little bit different. I was always bullied at school—much like my son, I was "different" (which was the nineties code word for any child who was neurodivergent and/or struggling with trauma), and I remember the feelings of hopelessness, knowing that I would have to get up every morning and face the harsh treatment of my peers, but there was very little I could do about it. Watching my son go through the same experience has been deeply triggering for me in many ways, not just because I have experienced the helplessness that comes with knowing your child is struggling and you can't make it stop, but also because of the feelings of anger and frustration that no one made any rational choices to support me back then. Growing up, my mom's response to bullying was to teach me to lash out, bully back. When that didn't work, she would demand meetings with teachers, only to shame me, getting angry and tearful because the teachers had been rude to her.

The constant lack of support and trauma was overwhelming. Not only has this experience been triggering for me, but it comes with its own fears and feelings of guilt—am I making this all about me, and isn't that like my mom? Why am I feeling this way and relating it to my experiences, when the focus needs to be on my son? I would put to you, if these feelings of shame and guilt crop up, that we are complex beings. We can center our children in these scenarios—they are the primary focus and need to be respected as autonomous humans with different reactions, feelings and experiences to us—*and simultaneously* be aware of our own lived experiences, and acknowledge and navigate the trauma we are working through. We're going to talk a little bit more about taking ownership and being responsible for your own triggers in the pages ahead, but hold in mind that *you are not a bad parent for being aware that your child's negative experience is triggering you.*

This last personal example is one that I hear often, especially with couples who have different parenting styles. My partner is a shouter when he's angry. It is something that we have discussed throughout the course of our relationship and it has been the source of many a disagreement. He's always raised his voice, and it's something he has worked on being mindful of over the years. However, when we had children I found that shouting at the kids? *Big* trigger for me. Growing up, my mom was a shouter, but she would also underpin a lot of shame around shouting and anger. Yes, she would hit me from time to time, and we were never short of vicious words being hurled or hissed through bared teeth, but shouting was her go-to and I hated it. I remember turning to my husband once and saying, "Do you understand that I would have a less visceral reaction to being hit than being shouted at?" That conversation was a big one for us. Being hit was a simpler thing for my brain to understand as a child. I was fortunate to never experience being beaten—one or two strikes and I would be sent away— but shouting could last for what felt like hours and would almost always be followed with silent treatment for days or a rapid U-turn as if nothing had happened, leaving me feeling shaken and unsettled.

When my husband would lose his temper and shout at the kids, this overwhelming urge to protect them would surge up in me, because on the inside I was seeing that little girl who was so frightened of being shouted at. Guess what? When I would lose my temper and occasionally shout, the feelings would be even worse and I would end up triggering myself. Am I like my mom? Will they only remember these moments when I shout? Why can't I keep my cool?

It is impossible to make it through parenthood without losing your temper on occasion. Children are frustrating— you're responsible for keeping them alive, while they do their utmost to make that as tough as possible. You are allowed to lose your temper, but that doesn't mean it won't trigger you. The major difference between my experience with shouting as a child and my experience with shouting as an adult is the accountability and repair that comes after. We'll talk more in depth about accountability and why it's such a fundamental part of cycle-breaking parenting in chapter 14, but for now, please know that there is power in apologizing properly and moving forward in your relationship.

Regardless of what yours look like, triggers will always show up for us. They are a normal part of growing and developing self-awareness, but they aren't discussed when we talk about having children. No one tells you to sit with your partner and say, "Hey, this is probably going to bring up some stuff for me." Even if they did, it may not be effective because we rarely know our triggers *until* they pop up for the first time. I have spoken to countless people who have been triggered by mundane experiences like their partners bathing their children—even though they have the utmost trust in their partner—or raising their voice over homework. As cycle breakers, our children are a constant floodlight on the shadows of our triggers, but with each trigger that arises there is opportunity.

Three-step plan for dealing with triggers

This is how I break down dealing with triggers for my clients (and myself!). This isn't intended to "fix" your triggers or stop them happening, but rather to give you the tools to work with yourself and your triggers, and to be more in control of the impact that they have.

Step 1. Identify the "what" and "why" of the trigger

I call this the "get curious" step. Once we know what a trigger is, we are able to be more proactive and mindful of it in the future. When you feel yourself becoming overwhelmed or having a strong emotional reaction to something, ask yourself why. What is this bringing up for you? Identifying the "what" and "why" of the reaction is powerful.

Take my above example with the birthday party—the "what" was "birthdays and parties" and the "why" was because I had unprocessed trauma from one of my early memories of birthday parties. There can be so many "whats" when it comes to triggers, but your answer to the "why" might be a little bit more elusive—especially if you don't have many memories from your childhood. If you find yourself in this situation, sit with the "what" and allow yourself to consider the "why" without judgment if it's not coming up for you. You might do this by saying, "I know X is bringing up some big feelings for me here. I'm not sure why, and that's OK. I know the 'why' will come when it's ready, but for now, I'm going to be mindful that X is triggering something in me." Move to step 2 and revisit when you're ready.

A note here—I have sat with many people when a trigger has come up for them and sparked a panic attack. While it's a horrendous experience in the moment, know that your panic attack will pass, and you can look at these steps after you've managed to regain control. You're not a machine and sometimes those feelings may overwhelm you and take control. I'd also like to remind you, as the late Dr. Áine Tubridy mentioned in her book *When Panic Attacks*, that you will not die from a panic attack, even if it feels like you might. Take a breath, and when you regain focus, you can consider your triggers in a safe environment at your own pace.

Step 2. Own the trigger

When we talk about triggers, we can often fall into the trap of allocating "blame" or pushing them onto other people with phrases like, "You're triggering me!" But our triggers are our responsibility to hold and manage. Frustrating, isn't it? We develop these triggers because of our life experiences, and invariably they aren't due to any fault of our own. Think of it this way: if your finger is cut, regardless of how it happens, it's your responsibility to ensure you don't bleed everywhere by either wrapping it up, seeking medical aid or popping a Band-Aid on it. You might need help, but it's your responsibility to seek it and accept it. Our triggers are the cuts that dig into our traumas, and as healthy, responsible adults we don't let our trauma bleed onto others. If you recognize a trigger in the moment of a heated discussion or an argument, you might take ownership by saying something like, "This is coming up for me right now, it's really triggering me and I need to take a few minutes to walk away and breathe, OK?" Take a few minutes to gather yourself and then address the issue from a calmer space. It might be that you recognize this after the fact when you're lying in bed thinking, "Ugh, why did that make me so angry/

guilty/upset?" and the "what" and "why" become apparent for you. In a healthy adult-to-adult relationship, discussing your triggers is important, and it might require you to go that step further and seek help to work through that trigger and whatever trauma it has brought forth with a trained professional (i.e. the medical attention for when you can't stop the bleeding on your own).

When it comes to our children, it's a little bit trickier. My daughter didn't need to know that Mommy had worked out she was super guilty over the birthday party because it reminded her of when she was a little girl, and her parents were awful. In fact, telling her this would likely be the opposite of owning my triggers, as it would encourage her to jump into that rescuer role and try to make me feel better, which it's not her job to do. In this instance, this was something I needed to acknowledge for myself, and either discuss with my own therapist or navigate through self-soothing such as inner child work or journaling.

When we're working out what ownership might look like and how to move forward, we can ask ourselves the following:

- Who does it benefit if I discuss this trigger?
- Now that I'm aware of this trigger, did I behave in a way that might need me to take some accountability and/or apologize?
- If so, is it helpful to the person I'm apologizing to if I explain the reason I reacted the way I did?

In healthy adult-to-adult relationships, we can almost always say that it benefits both parties to discuss triggers and have communication around what upsets us. If I let my husband know that something has popped up for me, be it within our relationship or outside it, he can support me and be more mindful (without being responsible for the trigger). With children it's a little more challenging—does it benefit both of us or just me if I explain this? Is that necessary? Well, it might be if you need to take accountability and apologize, especially if your reaction has scared your child and explaining will help them to let go of any fear, shame or guilt.

This is a great example of when we might need to own a trigger in front of our kids.

A client of mine, let's call her Ava, had a difficult childhood with a lot of emotional and instrumental parentification (see page 38). From around the age of seven she was expected to be responsible for her younger sister. One day, they were out for a walk and her sister ran ahead right into the path of an oncoming car. She was hurt, but thankfully not fatally injured. However, the worst part for Ava was the shame she felt at her angry mother's response. Even as an adult, her mother would make remarks about her being irresponsible, and say things like, "Remember the time you let your sister get hit by a car!"

Her mother struggled with her mental health and addiction, often leaving Ava in charge of her sibling until Dad came home from a day at work, but even then, the situation didn't improve. On one occasion, Ava's son, aged five, did the classic trick of wriggling out of her arms and running toward the park slides, right across the parking lot and *almost* into a reversing car. He was absolutely fine, if a little shaken, but for Ava the event opened the lid on a situation filled with unresolved trauma and panic. She was back to being that little girl, watching her sister get hit and fearing the worst. Ava shouted at her son and then, much to her chagrin, had a panic attack and ended up on the floor trying to breathe while her little boy sobbed. The guilt she felt for losing control in front of her son and frightening him was immense. Fortunately, Ava's friend arrived and took her little boy to play on the slides and swings with her daughter, while Ava took some time to compose herself. After thinking through my steps for owning your triggers, Ava decided to have a chat with her son and explain what had been going on. She told him, "Hey bud, today when you ran out in the parking lot, it really scared me. It also reminded me of a time when I was little and Auntie Sarah did the same thing. Our mommy and daddy weren't watching her, I was. I was so frightened! When I had to sit down afterwards, that is because I was having what we call a panic attack, which means I couldn't quite get my breath as all those biiiiiig feelings were crashing around me. It's not your fault that happened, OK? You didn't hurt me, I was scared for you and then some big feelings came up from when I was little. That is my responsibility to deal with. I'm sorry that it scared you. Looks like we both gave each other a fright today, huh? Can we agree to be more careful in parking lots, please? Next time let's hold hands, yes?"

Ava wasn't seeking to make *herself* feel better by explaining to her son why the panic attack had occurred or to shame him, but to help him understand that it wasn't his fault she had such a big reaction, and to lift any sense of responsibility from his little shoulders. Ava not only corrected her child's behavior and came up with a collaborative solution for next time they were in a parking lot, but she took ownership *and* committed to working on this trigger in further coaching and therapy sessions.

In this instance, explaining that you might have had some of your own stuff going on in the background of an already scary situation is to help your child understand why your reaction was so strong. More often than not, we explain triggers to children to alleviate guilt or excuse bad behavior, which is only helpful to us. Keeping those questions in mind when you're considering how you can own your triggers is a powerful tool to keep yourself accountable and work on healing.

Step 3. Do the work

Now that you've identified the "what" and "why" *and* owned the trigger, it's time to do the work. To go back to our cut finger analogy, only you can decide whether or not you need a Band-Aid, bandage or medical assistance.

A Band-Aid may look like addressing some self-care needs you've been ignoring that have led to you feeling burned out and becoming more easily triggered. A bandage might look like journaling, taking courses to understand your experiences or reading a self-help book to become more aware. Medical assistance is seeking the advice of a trained professional. I am a huge advocate for therapy, and if you find triggers are causing reactions that have a huge impact on your life and ability to function day to day, seeking professional help to work through your trauma is a vital part of cycle breaking.

Remember: we don't bleed our trauma onto other people, especially not our children. It is always your responsibility to navigate and heal your trauma. It's often the choice our parents didn't make.

Chapter 12

Listening to your children (so that they actually feel heard)

Has your child ever turned to you and said, "*Ugh!* You never listen to me!" Chances are, if you have a child old enough to speak, then the answer is yes. Listening is something that we adults, especially when we're parents with our own preconceived notions, aren't always the best at doing. I have this conversation fairly often with my teenager, who will turn to me and say, "You never listen!" To which I will reply, "No, I do listen, I just don't agree with you!" And we will go back and forth until eventually I will say, "OK, we're at an impasse, let's take a minute—but you still have to do your homework!"

Listening isn't really thought of as a skill, but it absolutely is. Would it surprise you to know that a fairly sizable chunk of the early days of training to be a therapist is spent *learning how to listen*?

Listening is not a skill that we're taught, and if we have toxic parents or family dynamics, I guarantee it's not one you've had modeled to you. In this section we're going to dip into some core listening skills, do some thinking about blocks to listening and talk about some effective ways to communicate so you're not at loggerheads. As an FYI, you can use this part of the book to help you in all areas of life, not just as a parent.

Listening skills no one taught you (but that will help you be a more effective listener)

Non-verbal listening skills

So much of listening and feeling listened to is about our non-verbal skills, such as body language and those non-verbal cues we overlook, like saying "mmm-hmm" and head nodding. An easy way to remember non-verbal communication is to think of the acronym SOLERB, which stands for:

Sit opposite the other person.
Open body posture.
Lean forward occasionally.
Eye contact (without staring too intently).
Relaxed body language—check those shoulders aren't bunched and try not to fidget.
Breathe—many of us hold our breath when we are nervous.

Keeping this in mind when having a conversation with your child, especially if it's a disagreement, can be helpful in displaying to them that you are present with them in that moment.

Silence (what my kids call the "shut up, Mom!" skill)

This is a part of listening that I think most of us struggle with when it comes to our kids. Growing up, many of us were taught that whatever an adult had to say was far more important than anything a child could input, and despite always trying to hear our children, we can often fall into the habit of talking over them or rushing to answer the things they say without giving ourselves time to process them. In addition to this, as parents we often frame our role as the "fixer" to our children's problems. I invite you to count how many times you use phrases like "I'll fix it" or "I'll deal with it" throughout a day; I bet you it will be quite a few!

Next time your child is telling you about something, do what my kids say and use the "shut up, Mom!" skill. Remembering your non-verbal listening cues, let them talk without trying to jump in and offer suggestions or fix anything. Just listen. It is important, of course, that we use common sense with this—if we're asked a direct question such as "How would you handle it?", you can go ahead and offer your advice, but otherwise, see if maybe you can just hear them out a bit, and don't rush to fill the silence with your solutions, but instead offer your presence so they know you're there with them.

This can also be an especially effective skill if you have a child who has a tendency to respond to "What's up, sweetheart?" when you can tell something is upsetting them, with a resounding "I'm fine!" If you have this child—I do—then responding to this with, "OK darling, well, I am here if you want to talk, OK?" and then either asking them to do a task with you, like cook dinner or play their favorite video game, read a book or just have a cuddle, can be a great way to offer them both autonomy and silence in which to hear them, should they wish to share their worries with you. It tells them "I'm here," without trying to force them to share.

Open and closed questions

While we're talking about that child who may be reluctant to share their worries, the types of questions we ask can have a big impact. Open questions are questions that require more than a yes or no answer, and they get you to open up. This might sound like, "What was your favorite thing that happened at school today?" or "What made you laugh at school today?" By contrast, closed questions are much more about seeking information; they can usually be answered in one or two words, such as, "Did you have a good day at school?" or, "Are you hungry?" I'm sure it's no surprise that connecting with your child means we lean much more toward the open questions angle. When I want to know about their day, I never ask my children if they had a good time or what they got up to, because they will grunt and reply "nothing." So instead, I ask specific and open questions such as those above. They will often frown and say, "Dunno," before launching into a tale about what they *do* know. Or I will follow up with, "Hmm, if you don't know your favorite thing about the day, what *didn't* you like?" And they usually have lots of things to tell me then!

Reflection

You might have heard therapists and coaches being referred to as a "mirror" to our inner self. A lot of that comes down to the way in which they use the skill of reflection to help you feel seen and heard. We can use this skill in a couple of ways, but think of it as pointing out what we see or hear. If your child comes bouncing up to you with a big smile saying, "Mom! Mom! Mom!" you might say, "Ooh, you look really excited!"—this reflects back to them a chance to share that feeling more deeply. You might see the reverse—an angrily thrown down backpack, slouchy shoulders and shoes flung from feet—and instead of jumping into, "Hey, what's up with you?" or "Hey! Don't throw your bag down like that!" we might say, "Oh dear, you seem really angry and upset." In this way we are reflecting what we see.

We can also use reflection in a more simplistic way, by simply saying the important words we hear. For example, your child might be talking to you about something that has happened today at school. They might say, "I don't like it when I play with Summer, she's so horrible!" And you might reply, "Hmm, she's horrible?"—you're reflecting back their words to them, and what invariably happens is they say, "Yeah! She did . . ." and then really jump into sharing with you what bothered them. You could just say, "What has she done?" But reflecting words back often makes us consider them more and feel more heard.

Paraphrasing

When we're listening to someone, paraphrasing what they are saying can be really useful in not just clarifying the conversation, but also getting them to think about what they are telling us. Whenever my son comes home from soccer games to tell me about whatever drama happened on the field this week, I will listen to him intently and then say, "Hmm, you felt that that penalty was a bit harsh. It was a dive, huh?" And he will launch into exactly why he thinks that, pouring out all of his outrage while I listen to him. Obviously this is a light-hearted example, but paraphrasing can be effective for all situations—it not only gives your child the chance to say whether you have understood them properly, but also lets them know you've listened, kept up and engaged in what they have said.

Are all of these tools essential every time we have a conversation with our kids (or anyone)? Absolutely not—it's for you to decide when you think it's appropriate to pull one out of the bag, just as you would with any tool in a toolkit. But practicing these different skills will improve your ability to listen and create a welcoming space in which your child feels heard.

What are your blocks to listening?

What stops you from listening to someone? If my child were to come home right now as I am typing, the following thoughts would stand in the way of me really listening to him:

- I'm not feeling well, I have a head cold (courtesy of his brother!).
- I've put my cup of tea somewhere, but then I got a text message from a friend about an upcoming date, and I can't remember where I left it.
- I've been sitting in this seat at my desk for hours with only a couple of breaks, and I really feel the weight of that tiredness after a day of working.

- I'm thinking about what I need to do for dinner, but I really don't want to cook . . .
- I know I have some paperwork to fill out for school.
- Did my other boy have a good day? He was worried about going to do a biking course he really doesn't want to do . . .
- My car just needed two new tires and it's cost me $400. What adjustments do I need to make this month to account for that?
- Did I pay Girl Scouts?
- I'm really warm, but because I'm not well I'm also cold, so nothing I do is helping there!
- The cat just used the litter tray.

See this list of silly little things that most of us have in our heads 24/7? These are what we call blocks to listening. Can I still listen to my son while I'm thinking about these things? Yes. Can I listen while I'm also doing dishes, making dinner or even tidying up? Yes. Can I make him feel valued and heard as effectively as if I stopped and set time aside to be present with him? No.

Combining the above skills and setting out some time to be present with your child will allow you to form a deeper connection built on trust and understanding. It doesn't mean that will always be easy, especially as our children grow up, but consistently creating space and listening without judgment or acting as a "fixer" lays a foundation for them to know you're a safe person to trust.

Listening and problem solving

Let's break down the idea of listening without judgment or trying to fix a little more, because if you're anything like me, you're probably thinking, "But I don't want my child to struggle or suffer, so of course I want to fix the problem for them . . . and they must want that too, or why would they come to me?"

How often have you spoken to someone only to find yourself really frustrated when they start offering you solutions to the problem? (This is me with my partner every time!) What we wanted in that moment was to be heard, to feel validated or just to whine a little, not to be told what to do. To put it another way, how often have you said, "Right! I'm going to speak to the teacher for you!" about bullying, homework or something that has happened at school, only for your child to say "NO! I don't want you to!" before storming off to their room with a "You never listen!", leaving you feeling a bit baffled—you *did* listen and you were coming up with the best way to sort it all out, right?

Yes, sometimes your child will want you to "fix" things (naturally this is most likely to occur when you simply can't), but often it's about building connection—especially when the problem is with conflicts in your relationship. As our children get older, it's natural for us to feel like they are drifting away from us, which can be tough for a cycle breaker. We've talked in previous sections about the type of parent you might want to be vs. the type you had, what that looks like for you and how you navigate the challenges, but nothing quite prepares you for that slow pull away that happens in adolescence. In these moments, it's important to know that by continuing to provide that safe space, even if your child doesn't want to take advantage of it, and listening when they do, you can build those bridges back.

I mentioned that the above "listening skills" form a core part of early counseling and coaching training. Another area of counseling I think we can take from as parents is Interpersonal Psychotherapy—Adolescent Skills Training (IPT-AST). This is a program that teaches communication and interpersonal problem-solving skills, specifically aimed at helping to prevent the development of depression in adolescents. It's noted in many acclaimed parenting books and widely used in schools by clinicians, and it focuses on six communication skills. I'm hopeful that, combined with your new-found listening skills, these will help you build on communicating with your child without being the fixer, but also help them to develop the skills to be their own problem-solver.

The six communication skills for IPT-AST

1. Strike while the iron is . . . cold?

We've likely all heard the saying "strike while the iron is hot," but with IPT-AST we're flipping this on its head and striking while the iron is cold. In real terms, that means picking the "right" time to communicate with your child. This one is especially useful when you've had an argument or had to be the bad guy who dished out some consequences, when they've stormed off to their room shouting that you are the worst parent EVER, and you've had to swallow back the reply, "You haven't met my mother!" Ask yourself, is now going to be a productive time for a heart to heart? When tempers flare, nothing gets done. The same goes for that afternoon they fly through the door sobbing because their best friend no longer wants to hang out with them or was unkind, or when your smaller child comes in from school ravenous and moody.

Striking while the iron is cold means taking a deep breath and regulating yourself enough to allow your child to feel whatever emotion they are feeling without trying to fix it or explain your point of view. It's a pretty tough skill to learn, regardless of whether it's with your child, partner, colleague or friend. It goes against everything people-pleasers have been conditioned to do, and let's be honest, those of us who grew up in toxic households are likely either recovering people-pleasers or still battling the urges.

Whether it means waiting for the after-school snack to kick in, giving them the chance to cry on the sofa for a bit with an "I'm here sweetheart, OK? Come find me when you're ready to talk," or even readdressing an argument from a few days before, give it time to settle and cool before you jump in.

2. Put yourself in their shoes (and let them know you understand)

Empathy goes a long way to helping us understand each other, but in order to really empathize with our children, we have to put ourselves in their shoes. That means not minimizing their feelings or comparing their struggles/experiences to our own.

Phrases like "it's not that big a deal" or "wait until you have bills to pay" tell our kids that we are on different planets—we don't get them, they don't get us, and it creates a rift. If your child is really upset because they can't go to a party on the weekend due to other plans, put yourself in their shoes—this might feel like a really small thing to you, but to them it was really exciting, *and* it might mean that they are going to be left out on Monday when all anyone wants to talk about is the awesome party Claire had over the weekend. It doesn't mean we say, "Oh well, forget our plans, you can go to the party," but it does mean we're able to see that this might have meant something bigger to them than just a bit of FOMO. Validating your child's feelings lets them know you see things from their point of view—i.e. you're in their shoes!

3. Be specific in your language

Specific language feels less attacking during disagreements or big conversations; it's also easier to address and be mindful of. When my teen is upset with me, I get a lot of "You always say that!" or "You never listen!", but what we've started working on is being more specific: "You haven't listened to me here" or "You have said X and it's upset me." I find that I do the same. I will say, "No one listens to me!" when I'm upset or feeling undervalued, but I then find myself faced with a family who all feel baffled as to whodunnit, with at least one of them jumping in to say, "Hey! I haven't done anything," and feeling hurt.

Being specific about what is going on is a really great skill for you to practice and to teach to your child. Below are a few examples of being specific:

- Instead of "I don't like your attitude," you could say, "It upsets me when you speak to me with that tone of voice. Can we try again?"
- Instead of "I'm so sick of your behavior!", you could say, "I'm frustrated that you've had another detention at school. Can we talk about what is going on?"
- Instead of "No one listens to me! We're going to be late now!", you could say, "I've asked you to put your shoes on. If you don't do it now, we're going to be late, and that will mean consequences for you."

4. Have solutions in mind

You might be thinking, "Didn't she say no fixing?" Well, we're not fixing, we're suggesting solutions to collaborate on fixing a problem! Remember the example I gave earlier, where you suggested calling the school over bullying, only for your child to declare, "You never listen to me!" and sprint for the exit? Let's look again but make some small changes that have a big impact.

You've waited until your child is calm (striking while the iron is cold), you've put yourself in their shoes and reminded them to use specific language to challenge the catastrophizing when they said, "Everyone hates me!" Now it's time to throw out some solutions. This might look like you saying, "Well, I've done some thinking about this and I want to see what you think about me calling your teacher for a chat?" Let them tell you if this isn't the right idea and follow up with, "OK, well maybe we can have a brainstorm for some ideas to help the situation?"

I'd like to note that I've used this example as it's such a

common one, especially with disagreements that really don't amount to more than kids arguing with kids. I'm by no means suggesting that if your child is being consistently bullied at school, you shouldn't inform the school, but sometimes we have to allow them the space to try and resolve issues without our intervention. This goes back to sometimes being that parent who has to make tough decisions, and if the bullying is consistent, you may have to explain to your child that while you hear and understand their reservations, the school needs to know what is going on to offer help and support too.

Sometimes solutions might require a little bit of flexibility from you, and that's OK. Don't be afraid to ask your child if they would like to share their solutions for whatever problem you're facing. It's OK to include them in decisions, because you've already created that safe adult net that supports their decision making, instead of placing it on their shoulders.

5. Use "I feel" statements

When we start with "I feel," we're talking about our feelings, which are valid, exclusively from our point of view. It's a great way to check yourself before projecting your feelings and thoughts onto others, especially if you have a habit of saying things as if they are statements of fact instead of feelings.

An example of this with teens would be, "You don't appreciate when I've cooked dinner or you would come home on time!" vs. "I feel really frustrated that you didn't get home at the agreed time, as I cooked dinner." The chances are your teen hasn't intended to upset you at all—in fact, they probably haven't even considered you (ouch, but normal!). And in letting them know that you feel hurt and frustrated, you're giving them the opportunity to communicate instead of defend. Teaching your kids to use "I feel" statements with you is a powerful tool in empowering them to open up to you. It takes a level of connection and vulnerability to tell someone how you feel, and that's what we want in our relationships with our kids.

6. Don't give up—it's a work in progress

Communication is a forever process, one we will get wrong from time to time, but a skill that we have the opportunity to constantly build upon. In working through these communication skills and teaching them to your children, you're creating a foundation—that does not mean you're going to magically have all the answers to every bump along the road of life. Yes, you will fall out with your child, you will be the bad guy from time to time *and* you will mess it up, but don't give up on constantly working on your communication, and don't let your child give up on building their communication skills either.

Chapter 13

Helping children to create healthy boundaries (and setting your own with them!)

Ah, boundaries—I know we have mentioned them over and over throughout the book, but this specific section is about teaching your children to set boundaries with people and with *you*. Yes, you. I often joke to my husband that maybe I've cycle broken too close to the sun, because no one calls me out on my BS quite like my kids.

There is nothing quite as confronting as your children setting boundaries with you, especially if you have never been very comfortable around boundaries, or have been taught that they are somehow selfish or unkind. It's tough to learn to set boundaries (see page 68) when you've been raised within a dysfunctional family dynamic, so how are you expected to *teach* setting boundaries to someone else?

The good news? It's significantly simpler (note I didn't say easier!) than you think, and the chances are you're doing it for yourself in small ways already.

A guide to teaching your kids about boundaries

This is the formula that I follow for teaching my kids to set boundaries—something I've been inadvertently doing since they were tiny! I might not have had the language when my first child arrived, but I was definitely teaching him how to set boundaries in small ways, even if I wasn't quite yet setting them for myself.

Model them

It's important to know that there are plenty of ways to model boundaries—which means all is absolutely *not* lost if you are still struggling to set them for yourself.

When we talk about modeling boundaries, there are a few ways we can do this:

- **Set them with others for yourself** (refer back to page 69 if you need some help, or check out the Resources section for some kick-ass boundary resources!) and let your kids see. This might look like, "Please don't speak to me like that. If you do, we'll leave" or "I can't speak on the phone right now, I'll call you later." It's absolutely OK to let your children see you setting boundaries—use your discretion on the subject matter, but I would urge you to consider that if your child witnesses things like you being spoken to unkindly, being berated or having to sit through hurtful comments, it's important for them to see you standing up for yourself if you feel able.

- **Set them with your children for yourself.** This is one that we so often overlook, but the truth is we do it all the time without even realizing and it teaches our children that it's OK to set boundaries! Things like saying, "I just want to finish my dinner before I come and read with you, OK?" or "I'm not coming outside to play soccer this afternoon, darling. I just want to sit quietly, I need some rest" have a great impact on teaching children they can say no to things.

- **Have some gentle boundaries around the house.** These are another way we model boundaries without realizing. Ever been to a friend's house and marveled at how their kids, even as tiny tots, seem to know not to climb in certain places or touch certain things? I remember a friend's house that we used to go to for toddler meet-ups was filled with breakables and it *still* baffles me that her kids would just . . . leave them alone. Well, that was down to her kick-ass boundaries. She'd gently but firmly instilled that the windowsill was a no-go zone, that the fireplace was not to be touched. Over time these things became totally unspoken and given. We all have gentle boundaries, so take some time to think about what yours might be.

Encourage them to set boundaries with you (and others)

This is probably the step that is the most obvious, but how we do it might surprise you! It's often an unconscious action once you get going, but many of us forget to do it.

Here are a few of the things that I do:

- **Ask/inform them! Empowering your kids to have a voice on matters is *huge*.** A few years ago there was a news story about someone encouraging us to ask our children for consent to change their diaper and wipe their bottom. That may have seemed a bit extreme at the time, but informing your child of what you're doing— even in these tiny stages—is a clever way to make boundaries a very normal part of everyday life from the very beginning. In this instance, I would talk through the process: "Hey, sweetie, Mommy is changing that bumbum now! Yes, make sure you're nice and clean so that you're not sore, OK?" The reason this hits a brick wall whenever it comes up in conversation is twofold: firstly, no one has made it through the toddler years without a toddler screaming bloody murder while you try to change them, so being told you have to ask for consent seems a bit ridiculous when you're going to be met with a resounding "NNONNONOONO!" from Stinky McGee. Secondly, we're simply not used to giving children *a voice* in matters that concern them. Informing them of what is happening and adding "OK?" isn't *quite* the same as asking permission—i.e. what are we teaching them if we ask for consent for things like diaper changes and then have to swoop in and ignore their no? But it does empower them to say no, or express their upset, which allows you to stay with them, offer encouragement and say, "Oh dear, I know you don't like it, but if I don't change your diaper, you'll be sore and it's my job to make sure that doesn't happen, OK? Nearly done!" This is an example of how to ask/inform at the earliest stages in our parenting, but we can do this throughout by saying things like, "Would you like me to cut up your sausages?" or "I need to brush your hair, would you like to do that in the living room watching TV or grab a book?" Asking their opinions for things, while staying in that safe and supportive parent role, is a big part of cycle-breaking parenting.

- **Help them build the boundary.** This is especially helpful in situations with family who don't understand or respect boundaries, especially those of children. Things like asking (see previous!), "Do you want a hug from Uncle Tom?" and then, if the answer is no, saying, "They don't want to hug right now. You can go ahead and do a high five or wave instead!" It goes back to leading by example, but here we're actively advocating for our children and teaching them how to advocate for themselves. Another example of this is knocking on their bedroom door wayyyy before we reach the teenage stage. My son will often say to others, "Hey, can you knock on my door, please?" or ask me to remind his dad and siblings that the door is there for knocking on, and he is entitled to his privacy! It's important (and healthy) for them to have those moments of empowerment and know you have their backs, even over the smallest things.

- **Practice together and/or be the space they come to if they need to discuss a boundary.** When children come to us with a problem, or to tell us they are feeling like they don't know what to do in a situation, it's an ideal time to talk about boundaries and help them to set them. An example of this might be a friend at school standing too close, someone tickling them when they have said stop, or even the language a family member uses around their appearance, sexuality or lifestyle choices.

Listening to your child, hearing them out and then using the IPT-AST framework above to come up with some solutions together is empowering for them, especially if they know you have their back should the boundary not be received well.

Respect their boundaries

This is probably the one that you're 100 percent sure you'll always be fantastic at . . . until you have to actually do it. I've said many times that nothing is as confronting as your child setting a boundary with you—but I also want to clarify that respecting boundaries as a parent doesn't always look the same as it might with a friend or partner. We have to remember that our children's wellbeing is our responsibility, and sometimes the boundary they set might not align with that. But, happily, we can put a few steps in place to manage these turbulent waters.

- **Talk, talk, talk.** When it comes to boundaries around things like devices, dating, relationships, drugs and more, things can get a little tricky. I remember my son getting his first phone and thinking about how I could both respect his privacy, teaching him that it matters (i.e. he's entitled to boundaries around his personal stuff), *and* keep him safe. We came up with a plan together—initially, we agreed that in the evening I could ask him to show me what he'd been up to on his phone that day, and we could look through his social media and messages together, and that I would know his passwords but wouldn't access his phone without him present. It worked for us, and on the odd occasion there were text messages exchanged that I thought crossed a line, we talked it out. He didn't feel like I invaded his privacy or took away his autonomy, and I could keep him safe. As he grew into having a device, these rules remained, but we found over time that they were never really used—in fact, he would come to me first if he felt something was wrong.

- **Explain what is and isn't a boundary and why things might need adjusting.** Again, this is about communicating and explaining things, without assuming your child will simply do as you say (or that they should just accept what you say because they live in your house). I've seen this in so many different circumstances, often around phones/devices and other relationships. I remember having a chat with a friend after her teenage daughter screamed at her, "You're not respecting me! It's my body, I can choose. You're overstepping my boundaries and trying to control me!" when she told her she wasn't prepared to sign a consent form for her to get a piercing. She felt baffled: after years of teaching her all the right language, how could it be turned on her over such a silly thing? Parenting and boundaries aren't always simple, and as children grow into adolescents it's perfectly normal for there to be pushback or conflict between your needs to protect or care for them, and their stretches for autonomy. I asked my friend why she felt her daughter couldn't get a piercing—what was the reason behind setting that rule? She said her daughter played sports and she was worried the piercing would get hurt. I asked her if she explained any of this and she said, "Well, I tried, but let's be honest, she just doesn't get it and I'm the bad guy here." I told her to be OK with being the bad guy, because sometimes you have to be. In this scenario, the best thing she could do is explain to her daughter that she wasn't going to sign her consent for a piercing because, as the responsible adult, she had to weigh up the risk vs. allowing her to stretch for autonomy, and on this occasion the decision was no. It was still her body, and if she wanted to do something that wasn't a potential risk, she could— like cutting her hair, for example. It's important to acknowledge how your child feels here: "I get that you feel it's really unfair because it *is* your body and your choice, but we have to be safe with those choices, and I'm OK with you being upset with me if it keeps you safe. We can talk about it more if you want, OK?" Will they still push? Yes . . . but this is where *you* have to hold those firm boundaries. See also school attendance, homework, parties and anything else where your parental judgment says no.

- **Ask yourself why and who.** It's important to be mindful of the whys and the whos when considering boundaries in parenting. Who benefits or who is at the front of our mind when we say no to something or help our child readjust/set boundaries? If we go to a family dinner and my family member is trying to force my child to clean their plate after they have said they don't want any more, who does it benefit for me to say, "Just eat a bit more so you don't upset Aunty Jill, please"? When these feelings arise, getting curious and asking yourself "Why do I feel the push to overstep this particular boundary?" is really useful. A part of boundaries is stretching for autonomy and being trusted and respected to do so, so consider the times you want to push back and say no to your child. Let's say my child wants to go out with their school friends at lunchtime, the school allows it at their grade level, but I'm really uncomfortable and I say no. Why? Who is in my mind there? Am I saying no because I am worried about their behavior? Perhaps I fear they might be hurt and there won't be any adults around? Who do I have in my mind and are my reasons fair or reasonable? What compromise could we come to that facilitates the stretch for autonomy *and* soothes those fears I have? Sometimes we have to sit in discomfort, just like sometimes we have to be the bad guy.

As I said, this is simpler than you might think, but in practice it is far from easy. Being a parent is tough—and I know that saying might weigh on you because it's something that your parent used to excuse their toxic behavior, *but* it is true. Parenting is filled with uncertainty, mistakes and compromises, but with proper communication and by working on those boundaries, you can navigate even the trickiest times.

Chapter 14

Accountability: How to deal with rupture and repair

After everything we have discussed so far, I think it's important to talk about rupture and repair—in other words, what to do when you get it wrong. For any parent, but especially cycle breakers, rupture is a scary thing that pulls up big questions like "Am I doing everything wrong?" or "What if they grow up and don't want me in their lives?" These fears are often compounded by messages from toxic parents and flying monkeys alike, who will shout, "Just wait until you have kids!" or "You're teaching your children to cut you off! Your time will come!" The truth is rupture is an essential part of any relationship—it's impossible to have no ruptures at all, even more so in parent–child relationships because there is no manual on how to be a parent that will fit every situation, and it is normal for children to push back against their parents often and loudly. It is repairs that are the crucial step in any rupture process, and they are so often overlooked, either because of society's messaging that to apologize to kids is to show weakness or because of our own fear of owning up to our mistakes.

Let's take a deep dive into how we navigate rupture and what repairs might look like.

The myth of the perfect parent

One of the common phrases I hear when I talk about toxic parents, estrangement or how I'm consciously parenting my children is: "You think you're a perfect parent." As you read that, it might bring up some uncomfortable memories for you of approaching your own parent, opening yourself up to further injury by hoping for some kind of understanding and validation from them about your experiences, only to be told, "Well, I guess I'm the worst, huh? You wait, no one is perfect!"

There is truth in this of course, no one *is* perfect. One of the hardest things for us to accept as cycle breakers is that we are going to get it wrong from time to time—we will hurt our children's feelings, make mistakes and there will be inevitable ruptures in our relationships. In knowing and accepting this, we're already one step away from that deeply defensive and emotionally immature mindset our parents had that to be criticized in any way was a personal offense. When people tell you "I'm not perfect!", more often than not it's not you who is expecting perfection or is frustrated with them for being "less than"; they are the ones who are expecting themselves to be perfect, or expecting you to buy into the narrative that they are. The phrase is used to excuse behaviors and minimize your feelings so that your parent doesn't have to deal with the root issue and be accountable.

Striving to be a perfect parent can lead to us being dismissive and defensive. We're often loath to acknowledge the resentment and defensiveness that can come with the pressure *you* impose upon yourself when you strive to be a healthier parent than your own. This resentment is not just of yourself for being a human who is flawed and gets it wrong, but can also be of your child for recognizing your failures and flaws, often loudly and when you are least able to face them. Striving for perfection is a slippery slope that we're often made to feel we need to go down, but it leads to nothing positive—if we're not feeling that crushing failure when we do mess up, struggling with resentment toward ourselves for having flaws and our children for seeing them, we're teaching our children that perfection is the expectation and anything less isn't good enough, and *that* is the very definition of continuing the cycle.

When we can acknowledge our mistakes, we can step outside of that defensive mode (which is often propped up by shame and fear of failure) and step into our child's shoes. Does that mean we don't feel that defensiveness pop up? No, unfortunately not—but remember what we discussed earlier about our inner child and teen, checking in with them, recognizing when we're responding in a "triggered" state and offering ourselves a chance to pause and consider. When you're defensive, who is responding? What is going on behind the defensive feelings?

I'd like to just note here that saying, "I don't agree with that" or disagreeing in general is not defensive, but rather part of a collaborative discussion. You can (and should, on occasion, as a free-thinking human) disagree with family and friends, especially your children. You can avoid being defensive by allowing them to have their say, actively listening and then—especially if you find yourself feeling like you want to

scream, "You're wrong! That's mean! I'm not perfect!"—
responding with, "I'm just taking a moment to think about
what you're saying because it's bringing up some stuff for me
and I need to consider that before I reply." I appreciate this
might seem somewhat far-fetched, especially if you are parenting a toddler or young child who is standing in front of
you telling you that you weren't kind because you shouted at
them after they threw a tantrum over the "poopy" dinner you
lovingly prepared. The idea of telling them you need to take
a moment and—gasp—validating that you actually were in
the wrong for shouting and you can see you weren't kind
might seem outrageous, but that is exactly when it's the most
powerful.

Your child's dysregulation is likely to dysregulate you if
you allow it to, at any age, especially when dealing with
conflict within your relationship or when they rub up against
those triggers we have talked about previously. Modeling to
your children, even at a young age, that perfection isn't our
goal, it's OK to make mistakes and that we are all flawed but
doing our best is one of the key elements of cycle-breaking
parenting. We can model this by holding space for them to
share their thoughts and feelings, treating ourselves with
kindness and compassion in front of them and vocalizing it
where needed and, possibly most importantly, being accountable for our mistakes.

Cycle breaker's toolkit: Considering apologies

I'd like you to take a minute here to just pause and consider the following—you can jot thoughts down on a piece of paper, or you can just think about your answers:

- What is your relationship with apologies? Are you comfortable with saying sorry, or does it feel like it's opening yourself up to being vulnerable? Perhaps you are someone who over-apologizes, even when you're not at fault?
- What was your experience of apologies growing up? Did you have a parent who never apologized, perhaps viewed it as weakness? Maybe you had one parent who didn't apologize and one who constantly did? Perhaps it's a little more complicated than that and apologies were just words without actions, freely said but not meant?
- How does it feel when someone apologizes to you now?

You don't have to do anything with this information, but raising your self-awareness around apologies can be an integral part of understanding and leaning into repair.

The importance of accountability

Accountable, *adjective* (from *Oxford English Dictionary*):

1. Required or expected to justify actions or decisions, responsible.
2. Able to be explained or understood.

One of the things I talk about a lot as a coach is accountability, and the importance it has in our relationships. I can say, hand on heart, as an estranged adult myself: accountability could have saved my relationship with *both* of my parents. It isn't just me who feels this way—far from it. This is a common theme I come across on a regular basis, both with clients and across my social media platforms, and it all points to one thing: *accountability is key in relationships*.

So what does it mean to *be* accountable?

It really sounds quite fancy, doesn't it? Why not just say "to apologize"? When we use the word "accountable," it can sound scolding and harsh—we often hear politicians talk about "holding to account" and it's always in serious cases of wrongdoing with dramatic flair. I've had it said to me by many toxic parents across social media that "holding someone accountable" means you're being judgmental or patronizing—how dare you?

Accountability is different than just saying sorry—that's a part of it, sure, but for real accountability there has to be change in behavior, learning, growth and empathy. Accountability isn't just going up to your child and saying, "Hey bud, sorry I made fun of you," and then going on to do it again and again. Accountability means taking ownership of the mistake you've made, using "I" statements, like "I'm sorry *I* hurt your feelings" in place of "I'm sorry *you* feel hurt," allowing yourself to be vulnerable without defensiveness and being prepared to make the necessary changes.

Let's take a little look at an example.

When Marie was little she was really close with her dad; people would describe her as a "daddy's girl" or say that she was the "apple of his eye." When she was around six years old her parents separated, and her dad moved in with the woman he had been having an affair with. While initially Marie would go to her father's house for visits every few weeks, her dad became increasingly distant and would often tell her he was going to see her on a weekend but then never show up, or he'd forget to call and check in with her as he had in the beginning. If she questioned why he hadn't turned up, he would make an excuse and say, "I'm very sorry, darling, I was busy, but I won't let it happen again." But it did. As the years passed, Marie saw her father less and less; they would have a chat on the phone every so often, but as Marie reached her teen years she became distant, often causing arguments or refusing to take his calls.

As an adult with her own children, Marie would visit her father a couple of times a year (though he never reciprocated). She wanted to try and repair the relationship by talking to him about how his behavior had made her feel as a child, and why they had grown apart and never really had a close bond after her parents separated. Marie expressed the hurt, feelings of abandonment and self-blame that she experienced as a young child, wondering what she had done to drive Daddy away and why he had stopped loving her. She told him about all the times she'd wished he would be there for her, or waited all morning for him to show up as promised, only to find herself bitterly disappointed. Instead of listening to Marie, her father interrupted her repeatedly with statements like, "Well, that wasn't my fault, your mom made it impossible!", "We've been over this before, you're dragging up things I can't change," "I'm sorry you felt that way. Divorce is hard and I was struggling. It wasn't because I didn't care, but you have to understand that I couldn't stay with your mom anymore, it was too much for me!" and, "*You* didn't want *me* when you were a teenager! It's not just me who is in the wrong here!"

Rather than coming away feeling positive, Marie felt like her relationship with her dad was even worse. It was the last time she made an effort to go and see him.

What Marie experienced is the classic dodging of accountability, not just when she was an adult but also when she was a child, when she tried to tell him he was hurting her by not showing up and asking him where he had been. Her father couldn't change historic events, *but* he could be accountable for them by listening and empathizing, validating her feelings and experiences and being present in her life now. Had he sat with her, let her share her experiences of him as a child and followed up with something like, "Thank you for sharing this with me, I'm so sorry I made you feel that way as a child. I was really struggling and my relationship with your mom made it really hard to come by the house, but while that might be a reason, it's not an excuse, and you were stuck in the middle of that. It was never my intention to hurt you, but I can see I did and I'm grateful I have the chance to be here now. I'd like to visit more often, and I will come to you too, if you'd like?" The feelings in Marie following that conversation would have been so different and, with changed behavior and continual communication, that relationship would have flourished.

Accountability doesn't erase hurt, it is the stitches to our wounds.

When we haven't had accountability modeled to us we can often fall into the trap of either failing to hold ourselves accountable *or* accepting accountability for things we haven't done. As discussed in previous chapters, you can still disagree with your child when they come to you about things—a brief conversation with my teenage son would tell you I disagree with him frequently over bedtime, school, homework and more, and I will tell him compassionately when I don't think I have accountability for certain things (like him not being organized on a morning!). Remember at the beginning of the book we talked about stress responses? Well, over-apologizing or holding yourself accountable unnecessarily are common signs of a fawning response, and refusing to be accountable for anything is a common fight response. It all goes back to getting in touch with that inner teen/child and working out what is going on for you in that moment.

The imperfect cycle breaker's guide to repair

My hope is that at this stage in our journey together you are able to see yourself as imperfect without feeling shame or fear. Perhaps it's a work in progress still, and that's OK. Be open to the idea that it's all right, important even, for you to make mistakes within your parenting, and be secure in the knowledge that the power is in the repair.

The formula to authentic repair

I have found that this formula works whether we are dealing with an in-the-moment rupture or a historic rupture that your older child has come to discuss with you (or perhaps hasn't, and you have had to take the steps to get them to do so). While this might look a little different in different contexts, the principles are the same. Our stages are:

1. Acknowledge
2. Validate
3. Apologize
4. Change

Step 1: Acknowledge the rupture

I feel this step can be broken down into two phases. Not only do you have to be able to acknowledge the mistake you've made verbally to your child, but prior to that, you have to be able to work through it with *yourself* so you can meet your child from your adult self and work through any challenges.

It might sound a little trite to tell you that you have to acknowledge the rupture within yourself first, but it is nonetheless true and often where we misstep and fall into the trap of defensiveness. You can objectively say to yourself, "I shouted at them because I was frustrated over homework and I need to say sorry for that," but if your heartfelt apology (something your inner child/teen never got) is met with a hurt child who isn't accepting and continues to tell you that they would rather work with their other parent because you're too mean, it's likely to be triggering.

This is where the power of pausing can be really useful.

Take shouting at them over homework as an example: when you become aware of the rupture (often when you notice your child looking sad, they start to cry or—as they get older—they shout back at you), take a deep breath in through your nose, counting to four as you do, hold for a count of four and then release through your mouth for a count of four. This is the box breathing we discussed earlier in the book (page 56). You can do this a few times if it's helpful. It might be useful to verbalize to your child, "I'm just taking some deep breaths because I'm overwhelmed and I need to calm myself. Give me a minute, please." At this point, it might feel like you've hit the imaginary pause button: everything starts to slow down and it feels like the wind going out of your sails or the releasing of air from a balloon. In conflict, pausing and stepping back from the situation is a powerful tool, but one that can be so tricky when we are in a heightened stress response.

As you pause and take a few seconds to calm your breathing, notice what is going on in your body. Are your shoulders hunched? Jaw tight? Perhaps you're digging your nails into your palm? These are all common reactions to stress and it's likely that your child is experiencing some of them too, so go ahead and try to relax those muscles as you breathe out. I invite you to consider what is coming up for you and why this situation has escalated.

I remember trying to help my son with his seventh-grade math homework, only to find myself feeling a really deep frustration that he wasn't paying attention and wasn't able to answer the simplest thing that we had *just* covered. Instead of telling him I needed to walk away for a minute and would be back (remember our chat about triggers), I stuck at it, huffing and puffing. I was being pulled left, right and center by my younger kids asking for snacks, I was having a stressful week with work, I needed to get cracking with dinner and he kept sighing heavily and looking at the clock to see how much longer he had on his timed task. I snapped, barking his name at him and following up with, "For god's sake, you're not stupid, why can't you just get on with it? You haven't even watched the accompanying video! I'm not here to do it for you!" His face scrunched into a scowl. My words hadn't been kind and, truth be told, they weren't about him—they were a symptom of my overwhelm. There was frustration because I hated math growing up and was regularly made to feel stupid by teachers and my mother, who would reiterate, "You're like me, math isn't our strong suit," so my inner child and teen raised their heads, feeling silly again at not getting a 13-year-old's math work. His disinterest in doing the work felt like yet another thing piled on me in that moment and I snapped at him.

In this instance, he used the boundaries that we talked about on page 204 to step forward and say, "All right! Shouting at me doesn't help, Mom, please don't do that!" This immediately gave me the sign that I needed to engage a pause moment. I replied, "OK, just a minute," and took those deep breaths, acknowledged to myself what was going on for me in that moment, how it had impacted him and where we were at.

Had he not set that boundary and challenged me, the biggest red flag that I had overstepped a line would have been the change in his body language and facial expressions. Recognizing the change in his facial expression, his body language tensing and his demeanor shifting away from collaboration to confrontation is all part of parenting. In that moment, I'd lost the connection with him and, without the pause and acknowledgment, we would likely see a stomp-upstairs-and-slam-the-door situation (which can still be repaired!). When I had taken a few deep breaths and acknowledged what was going on for me, I said, "You're right, darling, I shouldn't have shouted at you there." The way an acknowledgment to your child is phrased is essential. Naming what actually happened and stating that it wasn't acceptable is much more powerful than just saying, "I shouldn't have done that."

The acknowledgment part of any repair is often where we feel our most vulnerable. We are actively saying, "I did this wrong, I'm not a perfect human being and I've messed up." It's possible that there have been occasions when you have skipped straight to "I'm sorry" without really acknowledging what you're sorry for or the impact your actions have had. This is when "sorry" can feel a little empty, and we often haven't given ourselves the time to reflect.

It's possible that you, like me, were a parent for a time before you started to do the work on yourself, or if you're finding it challenging to hit that pause button in the moment. You might find yourself thinking over your parenting after your kids have gone to bed, and while this should never be an exercise in beating yourself up for the things you got wrong or the moments you felt you were triggered and acted in a way you didn't feel was right, it can be useful in helping us to reflect and become more self-aware as parents. I will never forget speaking to a friend of mine who is one of four children, with the fourth and final child being significantly younger than her and the rest of her siblings. We were having dinner one day, talking about parenting and how different children receive different versions of us as parents because we're ever-evolving humans, and she shared with me a conversation she had had with her dad recently.

While her upbringing was, for the most part, filled with loving and healthy connections, she couldn't help but feel that in some ways her parents treated their youngest child differently and with a kinder, more empathetic approach to parenting. She pointed this out to her dad one day, who looked her square in the face and said, "You're right, we were really different parents back then. I wish I knew then what I know now, because as much as we loved you and always will, we weren't as good at this parenting thing and made lots of mistakes along the way that were never meant to hurt you, but I think did more than we realized. We know better now, but I'm sorry we didn't for you." She was floored at how much it meant to her, this woman in her early thirties who would consider her relationship with her dad to be great, strong and healthy, to hear an acknowledgment that, yes, they were better parents now, and to receive a genuine, heartfelt apology.

I tell you this because, no matter how much you think you've slipped up one day, it's never too late to acknowledge that mistake and make a repair the next day.

Step 2: Validate the hurt

Validation is a key element of any repair. When we validate someone we let them know that we understand where they are coming from and that they matter enough to us for us to *want* to understand their point of view. In my example above, after I acknowledged to my son that shouting at him wasn't OK, I could have gone on to say, "That wasn't kind of me and you're right, it's not helpful," thus validating what he already knew and letting him know that I recognized and understood the impact of my actions.

I want to just note here that validation doesn't mean we have to fawn to our children and really berate ourselves—there is no lying down and expecting a kicking here. It is simply letting them know you have the awareness to monitor yourself, and in instances where ruptures occur over things that simply have to be done—hello, math homework—your validation doesn't mean agreement.

Step 3: Apologize and take ownership

It might seem a little simple to say "apologize," but so many of us miss the mark when we do. Apologies are often delivered with a caveat, but genuine, heartfelt apologies don't include phrases like "I'm sorry you feel that way" that essentially make the injured party responsible for the hurt you have caused. They also don't include blaming language or excuses like "I wouldn't have hit you if you hadn't pushed me to it!", "It hurts me more than it hurts you," "I only threw your toy in the trash because you wouldn't clean your room" or "I'd never have been so angry if you just . . ."

These tell the recipient of our apology that we don't really mean it. What we're saying is, "Yep, maybe I was wrong here *but* it's still your fault." You may say to your child, "It really frustrates me when you're not tidying your room like I've asked because I have to go in there to vacuum and, well, I'm tripping all over your stuff to get through the door! So, I lost my temper—but that isn't your fault. I'm a grown-up and I shouldn't have lost my temper as it didn't help anyone. Moving forward, how can we work together to be sure this doesn't happen again?" You're acknowledging the *reason* you lost your temper, but you're also saying you can see it wasn't handled well from your side and not using the reason to excuse your behavior.

> *"Explanations are not excuses. We still need to take ownership when we apologize."*

Often when we apologize to our children and own our part of a rupture, we reach a place of understanding and—if they have reason to—you will find your child owning their part too. This might look like you going to your child and saying, "I'm sorry that I didn't listen when you were trying to explain your side of the story about the incident at school today. I felt really frustrated that I got a call from school after we chatted about not getting involved in drama, but I've not been fair to you by just exploding. I can imagine that made you feel really awful and like I wasn't in your corner, but I am." In acknowledging the rupture, validating how they feel (or may feel, if you're assuming) and apologizing without blaming can often open the door for them to say something along the lines of, "I'm sorry I shouted back. I didn't mean to be rude, I just felt so angry as it wasn't my fault and the teacher didn't listen, then you didn't listen . . . it wasn't fair."

You might also get a grunt, especially if you're talking to adolescents, and I'd urge you to remind them "I love you, I'm here when you're ready to chat" and give them space or readdress it at a later date.

Step 4: Change

A repair is just a bunch of words unless it's accompanied by a change in behavior. The change in behavior might be a collaborative effort, or it might be exclusively from you, but it is an essential part of any repair following rupture. You've probably heard the phrase "all talk" to refer to someone who talks a good talk but never follows up with actions. To me, that is exactly what toxic parents do.

In my experience, cycle breakers have experienced one of two things: they either have a parent who would never (or rarely) apologize—and if they did, it was for show or to benefit their image in some way—or, perhaps more confusing, they had a parent who weaponized apologies. This parent would apologize profusely, spend a lot of time self-deprecating and making statements like "Oh god, I'm so sorry, I've upset you again, haven't I? I'm just the worst!", and thus manipulate the child into rescuing the parent by either pretending to be OK or allowing their parent to casually gloss over the change in behavior and accountability stages of the repair for fear of upsetting them further.

With these weaponized apologies, it can feel even more important as a parent yourself to ensure that change in behavior is taken on board. I think it's important to note that sometimes this is a subconscious reaction when we haven't been shown how to apologize and build repairs properly. Like all things cycle breaking, this is a process of "know better, do better," and if you have found yourself over-apologizing without following through with changed behavior or validating their feelings, that doesn't mean you are deliberately weaponizing apologies. What it *does* mean is that now you have the tools to make meaningful changes that have a lasting impact.

If your child says to you, "Please don't post photos of me online anymore, Mom, it upsets me," that is a fairly easy and simple change to make—you just stop, or you have a conversation with them about when/who they would be comfortable for you to share pictures with. If they are telling you that when you shout they find it overwhelming, but you naturally engage with that fight response we discussed earlier in the book, it's going to be a process and take time and practice. The most important thing with change is a willingness to do so and a genuine, meaningful and continued effort to improve yourself.

I think one of the most beautiful things about change is that it can be collaborative. In her book *Happy Families*, Beth Mosley discusses her four steps to improving your child's mental health: **notice**, **connect**, **validate** and **collaborate**. I feel strongly that collaboration can be a key part of building a repair in the relationship with your child. Not only is it empowering, but done correctly it can be a key factor in facilitating changed behavior.

Let's look at an example.

My eldest son used to really struggle to find the enthusiasm for getting in the shower. It would take a whole lot of nagging from me to motivate him to turn on the water, and even then he would often let it run while playing on a device, or simply climb in and sit down, only for me to end up losing my temper, storming upstairs and demanding he get out of the shower NOW! We would argue about it fairly often; it would rub up against all my frustrations and trigger memories of my mother shouting at me about wasting water, which in turn would bring about fear over being "just like her." It was becoming a bit of a vicious cycle.

One evening, after shouting at him again for sitting on the floor of the shower and not washing properly, we went through the stages of repair. At the end I said: "I'm trying really hard not to shout at you over this. I'm not really handling it as best I can and we don't seem to be getting anywhere . . . let's come up with a plan."

So we did. We discussed what I thought was fair: not sitting in the shower for 40+ minutes, remembering to wash, and not expecting me to be constantly nagging him, which adds to my own frustrations. He said he could understand that, but he found he lost track of time and he really liked the sound of the water running so would prefer to sit and listen to it, and he often just . . . didn't realize. It wasn't like he was trying to frustrate me or be unreasonable, he just got a little lost in his own world.

We came up with a solution, together: setting a timer for 30 minutes from when I sent him for a shower would give him time to get upstairs, turn the shower on, get undressed and then jump in and relax with a nice long shower so he could enjoy the sound of water *and* do the things he needed to. We later changed this to having two timers—one for 25 minutes to tell him to wash and get ready to exit, one to remind him to leave the shower.

This worked so well for us, cutting back on frustration and creating a simple collaboration we could agree and reflect on. It might sound silly to some, but this is a common struggle, especially for neurodiverse children/adolescents and their parents, and empowering our children to find a solution together is a great way to model healthy relationships to them.

A note here: trying to "fix" this issue we were experiencing without first acknowledging the rupture, validating that he felt hurt and upset at being shouted at, but also that his privacy had been somewhat invaded by me having to interrupt his shower time, and apologizing for where I'd made an error wouldn't have worked and would have felt like placing the responsibility onto him. In order to reach a stage where we could facilitate change *through* collaboration, we had to acknowledge, validate and apologize first.

Showing up as your parent? You're not alone

This is such a challenging part of growing up with toxic parents. Chances are if you're reading this book, you have dedicated a significant amount of time to challenging the generational norms of your family, tearing up the blueprint you were given and doing your best to be the antithesis to your parent—so what happens when you find yourself showing up *just like them*?

We're likely not talking about the extremes here—in fact, we've discussed how common it is to go to the polar opposite of our parent in order to avoid anything we associate with their parenting—but it is inevitable that we will pick up little things that we grow to dislike, or even hate, in our personalities because they remind us of our parent (even if we don't want to acknowledge that these things are there!). As a cycle breaker, those moments where you repeat phrases you heard as a child or you notice your anger simmering and lose your temper in a way that reminds you of your parents are extremely challenging and come with so much shame and guilt. Despite the shame, it's absolutely understandable—and expected—that we might pick up behaviors and traits from our parents that we view as undesirable (or even if we don't, we might fear and shut down certain emotions because of our associations with them). Remember that blueprint we're working so hard against? It's still our blueprint; it's still a part of our foundation.

The crucial difference here is that you're actively working against that blueprint, actively re-laying your foundations and making necessary adjustments, being introspective and accountable. Throughout this book we have discussed generational trauma and how these unhealthy relating patterns are passed down from generation to generation, impacting our genetic makeup and behaviors. It would be wholly unreasonable to think that after spending all of your formative years, and likely decades after, in these dysfunctional patterns, you would be able to break every cycle yourself. When you notice yourself doing something that reminds you of your parents, I'd like to gently remind you to take a breath, acknowledge it and move forward without being too hard on yourself.

Journaling pages

- What are your fears surrounding your parenting? Write them down. Now let's look at the evidence in your behavior and who you are as a person. Does it support the fear? How so? What changes can we make if yes?

- What did you need as a child? Jot down what you would have done differently to protect little you.

- Think of a time when you didn't show up as the parent you want to be. How would you do it differently? Let yourself know that you forgive yourself and you're going to learn from the experience and move on.

Section 4

Freedom to be YOU

In this final section of the book, we're really leaning into *you*: what makes you tick, who you are as a person and as a parent. We'll be looking into self-awareness and why it is so crucial as a parent and someone healing from a toxic upbringing, coping with guilt and shame, practicing gratitude and looking into your next steps as a cycle breaker.

Chapter 15

Stepping into you

We often assume that the most challenging part of being a cycle breaker, especially if that comes hand in hand with cutting ties with or distancing yourself from a toxic family member, will be coming to the realization that your family dynamic wasn't actually healthy. Well, alas, that's not the case. In my personal experience and working as a coach, I can tell you that the most challenging part of cycle breaking is really working out who *you* are and allowing yourself to be the person that you want to be. You're no longer restricted to being the version of you that suits your family system, nor do you have to follow their patterns of behavior in your parenting journey. What does that mean for you?

Well, it's time to step into your true self, and while this book can help to nudge you in the right direction, I want to make it clear that this is a forever path; we are constantly evolving and learning about ourselves, what we want from life and who we are. With that comes mistakes, changes and all the wonderful things that life can offer us if we're open to it.

Let's take the first step . . .

Self-discovery and you: Increasing self-awareness

Self-awareness is a fundamental part of being a cycle breaker and, regardless of how self-aware you think you are, there is always room to learn more about yourself. Increasing your self-awareness can help you navigate those times when you do something that reminds you of your parents, that doesn't align with the parent or person you want to be or that feels incongruent with your true self. Self-awareness can give you the opportunity to meet yourself on a whole new level, to learn more about why you do the things you do, the patterns you hold in your relationships and the core beliefs you have about yourself.

It can also be a huge part of helping us to navigate triggers within our parenting and relationships. Why does it upset me so much that my child doesn't seem to be grateful for the dinner I've cooked? What causes me to bubble up with so much anger and frustration when I don't feel like anyone is listening to me? Why do I keep my partner at arm's length and struggle to communicate with them when they have upset me?

With the awareness can come the change—because we can't change what we don't know about or understand! Let's take a look at a few exercises that can help you build that self-awareness.

Cycle breaker's toolkit:
Self-awareness using the Johari window

Johari Window

	Known to self	Not known to self
Known to others		
	Arena	Blind Spot
Not known to others		
	Façade	Unknown

This exercise is a simple tool for helping to increase our self-awareness and can help you to recognize some traits about yourself. The model was created by psychologists Joseph Luft and Harrington Ingham with the intention of helping us to consider more about ourselves, how we are perceived by others and the traits that we possess.

The Johari window is made up of four quadrants (in some therapy theories these are presented as your "rooms of self") and these are:

- **Open**—traits that are known to you and others. You would describe yourself as possessing these traits and people who know you would agree.

- **Blind**—traits that aren't known to you but others would use to describe you. Remember, these are people's perceptions of you; they might not be things you agree with, and that's OK.
- **Hidden**—traits known to you but that you don't show to others. These are the things that you know about yourself but choose not to share with others, consciously or subconsciously, or perhaps they are things you believe about yourself that are coming from your inner critic and aren't true.
- **Unknown**—traits that you wouldn't describe yourself as possessing and that others don't see in you either. This might be because you don't possess these traits *or* it might be because everyone remains oblivious to them.

To complete this task you will need to get a list of adjectives that describe personality traits, such as "funny," "clever," "brave," or "shy." When you have a list you're comfortable with, choose the ones that you think best describe you. Jot them down on a separate piece of paper. Now you can ask a friend, family member you trust or someone else to tell you which traits they think describe you the best.

Any traits that don't come up at all, that you think don't describe you and no one else describes you as, will go in the unknown section. The traits your friends or family describe you as but you don't see in yourself will go in the blind section. The traits you see in yourself but your friends and family don't will go in your hidden section, and lastly the traits you all see are in the open section.

What comes up for you here? How do you feel about the traits that your friends and family have selected that you don't see in yourself? It can be quite confronting sometimes, especially if they are traits that you have negative associations with.

What about the traits that you have selected that you feel about yourself but others don't see? Are they traits that could be considered negative? If so, what gave you the impression you embody them and is that true or is this a message you've been given about yourself?

Contemplating the results of a Johari window can reveal certain aspects of ourselves that we otherwise wouldn't have considered *and* any negative messages we have about ourselves.

Cycle breaker's toolkit: The three whys method

This is an exercise that is often seen in the corporate world. Originally known as the five whys, it was created by the founder of Toyota in Japan, but it has spread far and wide and is especially popular in coaching and for developing self-awareness.

Take a scenario or conundrum you face. We're going to ask "why" three times to get to a deeper understanding of what is going on. Let's look at this in practice:

Diana's mom made a comment about her child's

appearance after they had been playing outside all morning and it really upset Diana. Why? (1)

Well, when she was a child, she always had to be perfect or her mom would relentlessly pick at her. Why? (2)

Her mom was really controlling and very judgmental; it wasn't the only thing that she picked on Diana for. Diana was never allowed to be a child, really. Why? (3)

Diana's mom was worried about how others would perceive the family, and she projected this onto Diana and her siblings, making them question their self-worth and feel like they were never enough. The comment upset Diana so much because it really slapped against that inner child "not good enough" wound and she doesn't want her kids to be made to feel the way she was. Ever.

I want to reiterate, the "why" should always come back to you, and be about questions relating to *you*. For example, we want to understand why Diana reacts to her mom with such intensity, not why her mom makes the comments in the first place (although by proxy we've answered that one!).

The three whys exercise can also be really useful when you're dealing with parenting conundrums as your kids get older. Perhaps you're battling with them over a sleepover and you want to understand why you are a big fat *no* on them going, or maybe you're on the fence about them walking into town with their friends after school and you want to work out what is going on in your mind.

Give it a try and see what comes up for you. Find out the deeper why.

Cycle breaker's toolkit:
Life lines

Life lines can be a really useful tool for seeing patterns in your behaviors, relationships and life. They help us to build self-awareness so that we can step outside of unhealthy patterns, but they can be quite confronting, so make sure you take your time, find a safe space and refill your self-care cup.

On a piece of paper, draw yourself a timeline from birth to whatever age you are now. On this timeline, jot down any significant life events that have impacted you, challenging or positive, from birth onwards. It's up to you if you choose to add any notes to these events, but they might be things like "Started school," "Got married," "Had a baby," "Family member died," etc.

Remember that these are personal to *you*. Do you think the event impacted you? Then add it to the list—nothing is too small if you feel it had an impact on you.

When you've got your timeline, consider the following questions:

- Are there any patterns in my relationships?
- How do I feel about the timeline? Was it easier to notice/ focus on negative or positive events?
- How have my experiences influenced my life?
- What skills/knowledge/attitudes did I develop after each event? How did these help me move through challenging times, or make positive times more difficult?
- What core beliefs have these events given me? Are there any blocks I can see?

- What has been a turning point in my life? Has there been more than one?
- What values have been important to me?

Building self-awareness with shadow work: Get to know your shadow side

Psychologist Carl Jung, often considered the father of shadow work, theorized that we all have a self (our center, conscious awareness), a shadow (our hidden traits we have suppressed) and a persona (the face we show the world). The shadow self is the part of us that we keep hidden, often unconsciously, something that we tend not to present to the outside world and that we suppress within ourselves. We often ignore our shadow or ascribe to it traits we're taught by society are bad, harmful to others or detrimental to ourselves, such as anger, stubbornness or spite.

He also theorized that with light must come shadow, so the traits that we might consider desirable will also have a less desirable side that we will suppress and hide in our shadow.

Shadow work has progressed a lot since Jung's time. However, many of the core principles remain—and when you think about it, it makes sense. We all have those parts of us that we don't like, that we have been taught aren't "good" or to hide away. For adult children of narcissistic parents, these shadow parts are often misrepresented by the messages we're *told* about ourselves; they're not our true shadow. If anything, we learn to suppress more; we learn to fear our true shadow, because what if some of those traits that our toxic parent always accused us of having are true to some degree?

I remember always being told as a child that I was spiteful—even from a young age, my mother would talk about how I looked just like my father when I was angry, with a "spiteful little piggy face," and how my mouth would draw into a scowl just like his. I have always been fearful that perhaps that is true, maybe I'm just a spiteful person. I can now say, with confidence, I am far from a spiteful person—I strive to be kind; no one who knows me would ever describe me as spiteful, and if anything I have historically harmed myself to help or please others. Yet as an adult who has done shadow work I can see that I *do* have a spiteful side in my shadow. Guess what? That's OK. With that knowledge and acceptance of self, I can work with my shadow instead of feeling caught up in shame—I can understand where this has come from, how to manage it and what it means for my relationships and reactions, *and* find the light in the shadow (hard with some of the more toxic traits, I know).

Sticking with this spiteful shadow side—spite comes from a feeling of unfairness, when we believe we're justified in causing harm to another because they have wronged us (or we perceive they have), and we gain satisfaction from it. It often comes from a place of defense, becoming an offensive protection mechanism over time, and if we are unaware of it, we can allow the shadow to take over, which leads us to act out. When I think about my mother, I believe that a lot of her behavior was spiteful, but it was part of her generational trauma and done to protect herself—the phrase "I will hurt you before you hurt me" comes to mind. This became a pattern that she either chose not to or could not work with and integrate within herself to become more aware of her actions and how they impact others. I know that I can become spiteful when I feel insecure or threatened, and yet I choose to be aware of those thoughts and feelings, I don't judge them and I don't act on them. I choose to acknowledge them because while my shadow might contain elements of spitefulness, a trait I really don't like in myself, my true "self" contains all the opposites—kindness, friendliness and benevolence.

When we start to notice these traits within our shadow side, we can often feel overwhelmed, but this is where we can look for the positive ways in which we might utilize those traits, and what benefit they can have in our lives. This might just be self-awareness of the trait—or it could be something else. For me, knowing that I have spiteful tendencies in my shadow self gives me the opportunity to become more aware of my actions and why they are the way they are, and lean into that self-love that causes me to want to protect myself. If we consider IFS theory, where we are believed to have multiple parts and a core self, we know that we have "protector" parts who present with less desirable traits such as aggression. These parts sit "in front" of other parts in order to protect them because they are vulnerable or perceived as weak. Protector parts feel very shadowy, and considering this we can think about what that shadow might be doing for us—what might it help us to navigate or protect about ourselves? For instance, we discussed spite being my reaction to a perceived wrong, so perhaps I can lean into that sense of justice and use it to help me feel stronger when I've been wronged.

I want to really reiterate here that you do *not* have to accept or align with a trait that your toxic parent or anyone else pushed on you if you don't think it fits. I can say that I recognize my shadow trait of spite, but my mother would also refer to me as selfish and that isn't a trait I feel I possess—however, if it was, that would be OK to acknowledge and work with. The overall point to shadow work is to think of each trait as a double-sided coin—what are the positive attributes that might be on the light side, and how can we lean into them without shaming our shadow side? Going back to the trait of selfishness, the light to this would be a strong sense of self-worth, self-love, boundary holding and so on. We're not looking to excuse or enable negative behavior here, we're simply considering how we can make room for all of our character traits and use them in a way that is positive and helps us grow as people. Give your shadow a seat at the table of your core self and you will find a way to be the best and truest version of yourself.

Cycle breaker's toolkit: Finding your shadow

This is a simple exercise for starting shadow work and getting to know your shadow traits, and it can be really useful to do with a journal in hand.

What are your favorite traits that you possess? They can be anything at all—determination, loyalty, kindness or anything that you view as positive. Now let's think about the opposite of that trait . . . and there lies a part of your shadow! I'm willing to bet that if you really value kindness, someone who is purposefully unkind or cruel really winds you up, or perhaps if you are tenacious and determined, someone who is super laid-back, lazy and just doesn't have much drive will grind your gears.

Now you have the opposite of your favored trait, I'd like you to think about the positives of that shadow trait. Let's consider laziness—we would mostly all agree that to be considered lazy is far from a compliment in most societies; however, with laziness might come a sense of relaxation, being able to switch off, chill out and take things as they come. Some practices will refer to this as "finding the gold."

Remember that our shadow sits behind us, hidden. The idea of shadow work is to gain awareness of self without being judgmental or critical of ourselves. It's about reframing how we think about some of the traits that have always been perceived as negative, and allowing ourselves to be accepting of all parts of us.

Cycle breaker's toolkit: Noticing your emotions—a beginner's shadow work exercise

The simplest exercises in shadow work are often the most effective, and this is one of my favorites.

Noticing your emotions means exactly that—noticing what **strong** emotions come up for you with specific people.

Take a specific person and the way in which they impact you—it might be a colleague, a friend or family member. Their behavior really gets under your skin! Pay attention to the behaviors and emotions that bother you the most;

chances are they loiter in your shadow and you've been suppressing those sides of you.

An example of this might be a colleague who is lazy,
inconsiderate and self-centered. This sparks a huge reaction
in you, frustrating you beyond reason. This colleague may be
all of those things, but your reaction to them wouldn't be so
strong if you didn't also possess some of those traits in your
shadow. Compare this to the colleague who is blunt,
impatient and rude—notice how they bother you less? You
don't have to approve of or like the behavior of either, but
get curious about the behaviors that *really* grind your gears.

Be careful not to fall into the trap of thinking that because
you have a trait in your shadow it means you're "just like" the
person that upsets or harms you—you're not. You choose not
to allow your shadow to harm others, but it's important to
lean into it, find the light of these shadow traits and gain self-
understanding. With that comes a sense of completion and
you'll find that those traits no longer upset you the same way
they used to.

Entire books have been written on shadow work, and while
you can absolutely begin the process solo, I strongly advise
doing so with a qualified professional because our shadow can
be confronting, especially for cycle breakers. Both Jungian and
IFS therapies can be really great for shadow work as they follow
a similar thread, investigating and accepting all parts of yourself.

Discovering your core values

Whenever I ask a client, "What would you say are your core values?" they invariably draw a blank. We have already talked about the lack of self that so many adult children of dysfunctional parents experience, and people discuss quite openly how much we lose ourselves in parenthood. How does that look for us when we didn't really have a solid sense of self in the first place? Or if we did, we were taught it was shameful and something to suppress. We've talked about how so many people recognize their family's dysfunctional patterns after they have their own children, and how this compounds those feelings of losing your self—questioning everything you have ever thought, who you've really been all these years and what roles you've played. If you had asked me 10–15 years ago, I would have said I had a really solid idea of who I was, but in reality, after I had my children and started to recognize my childhood trauma, I realized I had no clue.

We can talk about lack of self until we are blue in the face, but one of the good things about recognizing that you feel you don't know who *you* are is that you have a chance to discover *you*. Not just you as a parent, but you as a person.

Considering your core values is one of the most effective ways to work out what really matters to you and the principles by which you choose to live your life. Social psychologist Shalom Schwartz developed the theory of basic human values, in which he theorized that there are ten universal values in life: conformity, tradition, security, power, achievement, hedonism, stimulation, self-direction, universalism and benevolence. Looking at these broad and vague terms can be confusing and open to interpretation. You might have pre-conceived ideas surrounding "power" or "tradition" but actually discover that some of your values *do* sit in that space. If we consider all values, they would likely fit into one of these categories and it's important to remember that no one value is superior to another—they simply are.

We have looked at our shadow and our self using the Johari window, life lines and the three whys exercises, so let's now take a look at your core values.

Core values table

Below is a chart of core values. I've separated them out by the ten universal values, but if you feel a strong pull to one of those values as a whole (security, for example), that's OK, just use that. Remember, there are countless core values, so if you would prefer to search online or to use some values that aren't on my list, you can absolutely do that!

Conformity	Accountability Courteousness Reliability Obedience Politeness Self-discipline
Tradition	Community Ancestry/culture Humility Legacy Loyalty Respect

Security	Approval
	Balance
	Belonging
	Fairness
	Harmony
	Health
	Stability
	Equality
Power	Authority
	Wealth
	Competition
	Control
	Leadership
	Fame
	Recognition
	Reputation
	Status
	Direct communication
Achievement	Accomplishment
	Competence
	Determination
	Mastery
	Success
Hedonism	Abundance
	Playfulness
	Humor/amusement
	Beauty
	Sensuality
	Pleasure
Stimulation	Adaptation
	Boldness
	Adventurousness
	Challenge
	Confidence
	Courage
	Creativity
	Vitality

Self-direction	Assertiveness
	Autonomy
	Authenticity
	Freedom
	Focus
	Honesty
	Integrity
	Imagination
	Independence
	Open-mindedness
	Passion
	Self-development
	Self-respect
Universalism	Accessibility
	Acceptance
	Spirituality
	Diversity
	Environmentalism
	Courage
	Inclusivity
	Interconnectedness
	Justice
	Peace
	Selflessness
	Wonder
	Wisdom
Benevolence	Connection
	Altruism
	Charity
	Compassion
	Generosity
	Gratitude
	Kindness
	Teamwork
	Thoughtfulness

What stands out for you here?

Let's narrow down the list of values—you will probably

want to grab a journal or a piece of paper for this. If you prefer, you could use highlighters or colored pens to mark which values matter most to you.

You might feel many of these values are things that you relate to, in which case pick five or six that you feel are an integral part of yourself. These will be the ones that jump off the page at you, the ones you instantly feel that you relate to on a deep level.

Next, consider the ones that you feel a pull to, but not as strongly—we're not dismissing them, but we're considering them less important to us than our integral five or six. You can have as many as you like that you relate to on some level.

Finally, we can go ahead and discount the ones that don't resonate for you at all.

Now that we have a list, let's think about the following questions:

- Do I live my life in accordance with the values I align with the most? If not, how come?
- Do I notice areas of my life where I'm not aligned with my values? What does that look like for me and how does it make me feel?
- What changes could I make to live my life more authentically (in other words, in alignment with those values)?
- Did I read any values that I didn't align with but that I felt I *should?* We've talked about how "should" is a scolding word and often comes from the expectations of others. So consider this: if you don't align with that value but you feel "I should be more like this"— what makes you feel that way? Who told you that you

"should" be that way and how did they benefit from that? Taking this a little bit further, I'd like you to think about some of the other "shoulds" that are present in your life and ask yourself the above questions. These might be things like "I should be thinner," "I should work harder/achieve more" or "I should call my dad even though he never calls and is awful to me when I do." Now I invite you to replace the word "should" with "could." How does that feel? Grab that freedom and let go of your shoulds.

Living as closely aligned to our core values as we can is one way to live for ourselves and lean into who we are. As you grow and develop as a person, your core values may change, and that's OK! Lean into those changes and accept them.

Chapter 16

Re-examining who you were vs. who you choose to be

When we grow up in a toxic family dynamic, we are often positioned in a role. We've talked about the golden child, scapegoat and invisible child roles that we can be pushed into by toxic parents, but now I would like to introduce you to Karpman's drama triangle and how we can choose to step outside of the roles we have always been assigned.

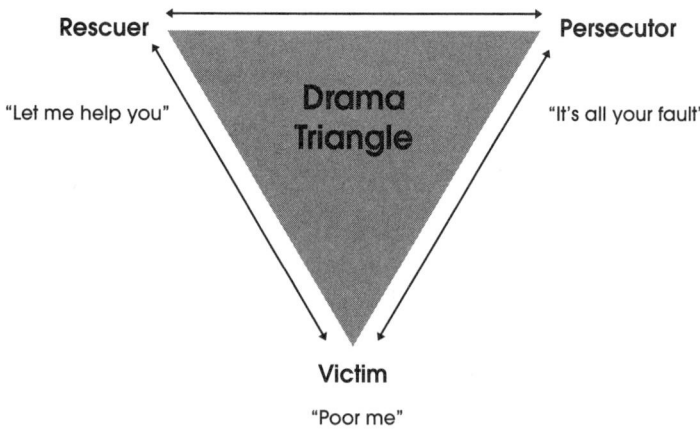

Karpman's drama triangle was developed in the 1960s as a way to investigate dysfunctional relational patterns, and how we behave/interact with others within dysfunctional relationships. Within the drama triangle, we have three roles in the power games we play with each other: persecutor, victim and rescuer. These roles work around blame, guilt and fear (similar to the FOG we talked about earlier on page 81, huh?). The model shows us how we play out these roles in our relationships, and indeed how others position us in those roles. Ever had a toxic parent tell you you're a bully/selfish/cruel, or heard the phrase "playing the victim"? Welcome to the drama triangle. Being sucked into these roles does *not* mean you are a persecutor, victim or rescuer—you can be an actual victim of abuse *and* be positioned as a persecutor or rescuer in someone else's game-playing.

We can also be in a drama triangle with ourselves. For instance, we might berate ourselves for being stupid and useless if we miss an appointment (persecutor), or we may complain about feeling stuck and unable to get out of our current job, saying, "I don't have a choice!" without actively applying for other jobs and being proactive (victim). If you are the person who is constantly doing everything for everyone in your family and feels underappreciated, undervalued and resentful, you might have a natural inclination to slip into rescuer mode.

Let's take a deeper look at the different roles.

Persecutors

A persecutor's role in the triangle is to blame. Persecutors are often aggressive (both passive and openly), angry and critical. This role says, "I don't respect you, the way you think or feel and I'm going to just think about myself and *my* needs. I'm taking charge and we do things my way." People stuck in this role can be judgmental, bullying and demanding. We often see ourselves being pushed into this role by a toxic parent who insists they are a victim and you are nothing more than a cruel person trying to hurt them.

Rescuers

Rescuers are there to provide *temporary* relief to a situation or person. This role says, "I don't trust others to fix or solve a problem, so I will have to do it for them!" Rescuers can be engulfing, self-sacrificing and fawning and are commonly considered people-pleasers, lowering their boundaries for others because they don't want to cause harm or upset, even when they might need to. They are the fixers—many parentified children will recognize having played the role of "rescuer" in their parent's drama triangle. When rescuers give and give they often become resentful, overwhelmed and step into a victim or persecutor role.

Victims

A victim says, "I can't" and believes that life is something being done *to* them. They don't accept responsibility and they seek out a rescuer to fix things for them, or blame a persecutor for their lot in life. They view themselves as "powerless," but they are often manipulative, and also work with blame and guilt. When a victim doesn't have their need to be "rescued" fulfilled by someone else (or a persecutor to blame) they can often step into the role of persecutor themselves.

Consider the roles you play or have been positioned as in your various relationships—and don't forget, you can (and will) move around the drama triangle over time. Shall we look at an example?

Annie's mom is often very thoughtless when she makes comments about Annie. She's also a gossiper and Annie hates it. It's hurtful and unnecessary, but Annie often feels like she can't say anything because it's her mom and she doesn't want to cause drama. **This is Annie's victim mode**—she also happens to be an *actual* victim of her mother's behavior, but we're setting that aside to look at the role she's playing. That doesn't diminish or dismiss the hurt Annie feels; however, it's Annie's choice not to set boundaries and to continue to avoid the drama with an "I can't" mentality that keeps her in the victim role in this drama triangle.

Annie is having lunch with her mom, her daughter and her partner. Annie's mom makes a comment about Annie getting a "real job" now that her daughter is a toddler, even though Annie has been successfully freelancing for months. Annie feels hurt and upset and doesn't respond—though she doesn't stand up for herself either.

Annie's mom picks up on the response and says, "Oh for god's sake, Annie, stop being so sensitive, I was just asking! You can't expect others to always pay your way!" **This scolding language is classic persecutor**—she blames Annie for the change in mood, instead of taking some responsibility for how her words have impacted the situation.

Annie looks like she is about to cry and says, "It's just hurtful, Mom. I'm not expecting anyone to pay for me and I contribute. Just because I don't earn as much doesn't mean I'm not working!"—this is a surprise to her mom; after all, Annie usually wouldn't say anything.

This is what happens when people in a victim role start to reclaim some of their power.

Annie's mom looks to Annie's partner and says, "Oh for goodness' sake, how do you put up with her? She's always so sensitive—and now look, she's spoiled the lunch I have been so looking forward to." **Annie's mom has switched to victim mode**, and she's inviting **Annie's partner to come into the triangle as the rescuer.** Annie's partner looks baffled and says, "Look, let's all take a breath, OK? I'm sure your mom didn't mean it that way, sweetheart, and we don't want to spoil lunch. Let's just move on." **Annie's partner has indeed stepped into rescuer mode** (more than likely without any intention to do so!), leaving Annie feeling invalidated and isolated. Annie snaps, "Great, thanks for the support!" **Annie has now stepped into persecutor mode.** Annie feels really embarrassed and upset, but she decides to try to appease her mom, agreeing to look for "normal work." She apologizes for her outburst and spends the rest of the lunch trying to make her mom happier with her. **Annie is playing rescuer to her mother's victim** (even though she didn't do anything wrong and was actually the wounded party!).

This is the pattern of Annie and her mother's relationship. Annie is trapped in a continual cycle and it's easy to see how. You're given an invitation to play a role—Annie can either try to appease her persecutor mother and become a rescuer, snap back and be maneuvered into a persecutor role *or* become a victim and not stand up for herself.

Take a minute to think about your relationships in which you notice dysfunction. Which role do you feel the strongest pull toward? What drama triangles are you caught in?

When we have these patterns and we're caught in drama triangles, they become our norm and there is comfort in the familiar, even if it's toxic or dysfunctional. We often create drama triangles within our other relationships—even with our children—because we have learned that role as a child. So how do we stop?

Let's look at the winner's triangle.

The winner's triangle was developed in the 1990s by Acey Choy to show how we can ditch the toxic patterns of relating and step into healthier ones. Where the drama triangle relies on blame, guilt and dismissing others' worth, the winner's triangle builds upon our strengths and helps us support one another. In a winner's triangle the three roles are rebranded as challenger/assertive, coach/caring and creator/vulnerable.

Challenger/assertive

In this role, a person leans in to being assertive—they actively seek their needs being met, but not at the detriment of others. They use their energies to solve problems—not be one! The skill in this role is being able to identify what your needs are and negotiating having them met (even in situations with someone really pushing your boundaries). A person in this role will assert boundaries, ask for what they need and find a way to get it without shaming, blaming or guilting others.

Coach/caring

Replacing the rescuer role, the coach (i.e. caring role) will ask, "What do you need?" instead of assuming they know best and can do a better job than others. They are boundaried and take responsibility for their own feelings; they don't do things that make them uncomfortable to please others, only offering their help and support where appropriate.

Creator/vulnerable

Creators can acknowledge that they are going through a tough time but they sit in their power, actively seeking solutions and being accountable. Where the victim in the drama triangle will say, "I can't," the creator says, "I can." They know when to reach out for help (hello, coach) and seek support, but they are confident in their own abilities.

So let's go back to Annie and consider the scenario if she stepped out of the drama triangle her mother was forcing and we had a winner's triangle at play. Remember, we can't control toxic people, so I'm going to leave Annie's mom in her persecutor role.

Annie's mom is still thoughtless and makes unkind comments that really hurt Annie's feelings, but recently Annie has been learning about boundaries and the drama triangle, and she can see her mom's games for what they are. She's not going to play. Annie, her daughter and her partner are out for lunch with Annie's mom when her mom starts to make remarks about Annie getting a job: "I just think you have to contribute, Annie. It's not fair that you're at home all day. I mean, what could you possibly be doing?" It's a clear attack, with her mother retaining her toxic behavior patterns and inviting Annie into the drama triangle. Annie takes a deep breath and says, "Mom, it really upsets me when you speak to me like that. I've explained to you that I'm working freelance, and it's hurtful that you think I just sit around all day when I'm not only working but being with our daughter. Please don't bring this up again. If you do, I will leave."

Annie's clear and concise boundary makes her a challenger/assertive. She's stepped away from the drama and taken control of the situation without being unkind or using blame, shame or guilt. Annie has asked for her needs to be met and declined her mother's invitation to play games. Annie's mom is shocked and splutters, "Don't be so ridiculous! Annie, you are embarrassing me. How dare you say that to me?" **Annie's mom is still in her persecutor role**, refusing to acknowledge her behavior and trying to pass the blame onto Annie, with a good dollop of shame for measure. Annie calmly responds, "No, Mom, I'm not being ridiculous, I'm asking you to have some respect for me. I won't engage in an argument with you here. I have asked you not to bring up my work or speak to me the way you did. If you can't do that,

I will leave." **Again, a clear refusal to be drawn in, staying in the challenger/assertive role.**

Annie's partner offers a gentle smile that lets her know they are here if she needs some support, but they can see that Annie has got this—**they don't need to jump in as a rescuer.** Annie's mom tests that and says, "Does she speak to you like this?! Annie, you're being so hurtful!" This is a **role switch from persecutor to victim, but she is still sitting firmly in the drama triangle and using blame and guilt** as weapons. Annie's partner replies, "I don't wish to be dragged into this. If Annie is uncomfortable, we will leave." They are clearly **refusing to be drawn into the drama triangle, instead remaining in a caring/coach role** and conveying the message, "I'm here if you need me, but this is your fight and I don't need to save you from your mom or make anyone comfortable."

As with a lot of toxic parents, Annie's mom refuses to adjust her behavior, switching between victim and persecutor modes to try to elicit a rescuer response from Annie. Annie stands up and says, "Mom, I've asked you to stop behaving this way and you can't respect that, so we're going to leave. I will get in touch with you in a few days to see if we can talk and find a better way to communicate with each other." Annie, her partner and her daughter leave.

When they drive home **Annie's partner asks if she'd like to talk (caring/coach role)** and Annie says yes, she's really hurt and would like to talk about a way forward (and have a hug!). This is **Annie leaning into her vulnerable/creator role—she knows she needs some support and can ask for it.**

She isn't saying, "Fix this for me," she's saying, "Can you sit with me, support my emotional needs and we will find a solution together?"

When you recognize that you are stuck in a drama triangle you *can* choose to step outside of it and create a winner's triangle instead. You might not have three people in your scenario, but as we've already discussed, you can move through all of the roles with yourself, with just one other person or as a group, and the roles are fluid.

I'd like to take a moment to point out that many of us have been positioned as persecutors in family disputes, or perhaps we have played golden child roles within our family dynamics growing up and caused harm to others ourselves. You have a choice, and you can forgive yourself for those past roles that you played and the behavioral lessons you learned throughout your childhood. We love the saying "know better, do better" in the cycle-breaker community—step into the knowledge of who you *choose* to be; don't allow who you were when you were surviving to hold you back with the reins of shame.

Chapter 17

Guilt, shame and you

Guilt and shame are often talked about interchangeably, but they are not the same thing. Guilt is something that we feel as a healthy, normal reaction to our actions. Think of Jiminy Cricket, sitting on your shoulder and letting you know you've messed up: guilt is our conscience being our guide to help us fulfill our true potential. In an article on her website, Brené Brown wrote that guilt is "adaptive and helpful—it's holding something we have done or failed to do up against our values." When we're raised within healthy dynamics, we can separate what is ours to hold guilt over and what is someone else's responsibility. In a dysfunctional dynamic, guilt becomes blurred with shame.

Shame is quite different from guilt; shame is something done *to* us, not something that comes from within us. We feel shame when we believe that we are flawed, unworthy of love and belonging. Shame pervades the body and mind, causing intense psychological pain—it's neither helpful nor productive. Shame is a feeling that we are taught—shame over our bodies, behaviors, likes, dislikes . . . everything. Shame has masqueraded as mom guilt, it's kept us in toxic relationships and taught us we are never going to be enough. Shame is often a weapon in a toxic household, wielded to pull you into line or make you feel like *you* are the problem, creating those internalized negative self-beliefs.

Almost every client I have worked with has said something along the lines of, "I feel so guilty I'm not taking my parent's calls, but I can't cope with them anymore. Their behavior is awful, but I feel like I have to keep in touch with them. They are my parent! It makes me feel like the worst person in the world to cut ties." That isn't guilt but shame—and how do we know the difference? Shame makes us feel inherently unworthy, so when we choose ourselves, *we feel like we have done something wrong*, which is how we can confuse it with guilt.

Considering shame using multiplicity of self

Shame is often the core emotion that causes a lot of our others—anger, defensiveness, fear, self-hate—to step in front of it and protect it. In IFS theory, shame would be considered an "exile" part of ourselves, a part we have abandoned. Think of our inner child, or even our shadow—shame is a part of ourselves that we suppress, push away and "exile" (hence the name) to the very depths of our true self. Sometimes shame can become what we would consider a "manager" in IFS—it protects a more vulnerable part of ourselves and we internalize it, becoming our own worst critic and embodying the voices we hear. As we touched on in the last chapter with shadow work, when we suppress a part of ourselves or we refuse to acknowledge it, it finds a way to act out—whether that's attacking us or others. I'd like you to imagine the following example; you can close your eyes to visualize it if it helps.

Imagine a young child. They are playing outside in the yard and come back to their parent for a snack. Young children mostly act from a place of true self—they don't have the same fears, worries or self-doubts that we have been taught to hold as parts of us.

As they toddle back over to their parent, expecting to be met with a smile, their parent loses their temper and says, "Oh my god, look at the state of you, you're disgusting. UGH, I can't leave you for five minutes. You make me so angry! Do you do this to upset me?! I'm going to have so much laundry to do. You are such a pain!" Can you imagine how sad and hurt that child might be, how they may feel like they have done something terribly wrong and internalize that feeling? It's the first time they have ever been made aware that playing the way they were was going to upset their parent.

The parent in this scenario has essentially handed their child a metaphorical seed of shame to bury into their personality.

Now imagine the child older, say 10 or 11 years old. Their personality is developing and they are learning all of the ways in which society tells us to hide parts of ourselves. They have developed a sense that their parent really doesn't like them by now, and after constant incidents like the one when they were small, shame has taken root as a part of them. On this occasion they are walking home with a report card, and instead of showing pride in and encouragement for their grades, their parent tells them it's not good enough, that they are pathetic and stupid. Can you imagine the feeling of that shame again? It's like a wound festering away inside of them.

If they try to appease or defend, they will face harsh consequences, so often their only option is to turn that shame inwards and push it down as much as they can. This is how it becomes an "exiled" part of ourselves.

These messages compound over time, and there are several ways our shame may manifest. Our key goal is always the same: to protect the vulnerable part of us and never again feel that way.

Developing an inner critic (the two-part internal shame cycle)

Our shame might develop into an inner critic; we mimic the voice of our external shamer in order to protect the hurt part of ourselves and internalized negative self-talk that truly believes we are unworthy. We start to shame ourselves—judging our appearance, our likability, our intelligence and more. The vulnerable, shamed part of us hides behind an aggressive self-critic to protect us from being flooded with feelings of unworthiness again. We become someone who lacks boundaries, fears confrontation, people-pleases and struggles to identify our true self. The message is, "If I squash myself down, if I behave differently and become small, I will be lovable." We attack ourselves and blame ourselves using shame, developing two parts of ourselves—the shamer and the shamed.

Because of this, we often have an untrusting side, are perhaps avoidant or anxious in our relationships and constantly strive to belong, even though we're never really sure we do.

The overall goal and message here: "I must never again feel this way, so I will make sure I fall in line with expectations to avoid it."

Externalizing shame (no, *you're* the problem, even when you're not)

Sometimes, shame continues to be squashed but manifests as anger and defensiveness, which we externalize to protect those vulnerable feelings of shame. Shame hides behind anger, causing us to lash out at others, be defensive and struggle to maintain relationships. We believe everyone is out to get us, and often refuse to let people get too close. We might even become a shamer of others, aggressively lashing out and always believing that we aren't the problem (even when sometimes we are!). If you think about your relationships, have you ever noticed that you've become defensive and oppositional when your partner or a friend has tried to talk to you about something you have done that has upset them? Perhaps you've ended up in a massive argument because you couldn't meet them in a head space that wasn't triggered and aggressive. This can even extend to people who have become the abuser themselves, hiding their own shame and feelings of inadequacy behind aggression, bullying or cruelty. As always, a gentle reminder that knowing this doesn't excuse this behavior, but it gives us a reason and an opportunity to do better.

The overall goal and message: "I will never again be the victim. My anger is a wall and you can't hurt me."

Let's look at some scenarios.

You're standing in front of the mirror doing your hair and your inner critic starts up: "I am so fat! I am so ugly, honestly, no one will want me now," etc. . . . . Think about what your inner critic gains from this. When you were younger, you were bullied at school and always told you were "fat and ugly." You feel hurt and shame. You develop an inner critic who has taken on the role of shamer because if you *just* lost weight, *just* looked a bit prettier, *just* put more effort in, you would never feel that way again.

Your friend comes to you and says, "Hey, that joke you made about me really hurt my feelings. I'm sure you didn't mean to, but it wasn't very kind and I didn't find it funny." You haven't intentionally hurt your friend, but you feel that shame being prodded, so anger and defensiveness jump in. You reply, "Oh, get a grip, it was only a joke! You're no fun anymore." You deflect from those feelings of shame by becoming an aggressor, because if you acknowledge that you've hurt someone, you will have to sit with the discomfort, and your system says "never again."

Whether our shame becomes an internalized narrative that eats away at us, or something that we bury and replace with anger, shame is the emotion we're not processing. We develop protectors to help us avoid processing it, and whether we're attacking ourselves or others, shame is a weapon best laid down.

What aligns with you here? Perhaps you've noticed that you externalize your shame, or maybe your inner critic has been carrying on for too long and it's time to address the old wounds.

How we address and release shame

Addressing our shame takes time, and we don't always get to jump straight to it. When we recognize that we have "exiled" a part of us (i.e. squished it down and hidden it within), it's really tough to get to, and the best way is to start slowly, moving through the parts of yourself that are standing in front of your shame.

Make friends with your inner critic

I know, I know, they aren't very nice, and it can feel a bit like making friends with the school bully, but alas I've yet to find another way to get them to back off and cut you some slack.

Thinking of your inner critic as a totally separate person within you, much like that inner child we talked about earlier (page 137), can be a really effective way of separating them from yourself and allowing you to engage with them. You might feel more comfortable writing this out, speaking into a mirror or just having a cup of tea while you have the conversation in your head. Be patient with yourself—it takes time and practice to get your inner critic to back off and stop protecting that shamed and hurt part lying underneath.

Notice when your inner critic is popping up. Perhaps they are picking over a mistake you made at work, telling you you shouldn't eat a certain food or accusing you of being a bully when you set boundaries with your toxic parent.

Acknowledge them—you might want to say, "Hello, inner critic, I see you."

Consider why they are here. What does this inner critic

gain from making you feel awful here? What are they trying to protect you from? If it's the mistake at work they are picking at you over, perhaps the goal is to keep you from feeling those feelings of shame and rejection that come with being told you're not good enough or you're failing. If they're shaming you for eating something, perhaps they are trying to avoid you feeling like you do when your parent comments on your weight. If they are accusing you of being a bully or cruel for setting boundaries, consider where that message came from—are they trying to protect you from the consequences you faced as a child when you tried to set boundaries? Or maybe you've always been told boundaries are cruel and you've internalized that message, so your inner critic is trying to protect you from being shamed, rejected and hurt by your parent's anger or abuse.

Thank and reassure them. This bit often feels a little odd when you first begin, but we can say something like, "Hey, inner critic, I see you—I know you're trying to keep me safe from feeling like I am failing or not good enough because I made that mistake at work, but I'm OK. I know what I need to do now and I've got this, you can stand down." You might say something like, "Hi, inner critic, I can see you're trying to stop me from feeling how I did when I was younger and my parent would comment on my body and weight, but I don't need you to do that anymore. I'm OK, I've got this, and I can enjoy food without feeling shameful." You might say something like, "Ah, inner critic, I see you and I really appreciate you trying to keep me safe from my dad's wrath, but you know what? I know that I'm allowed to set boundaries and I've given myself permission to do it without shame or fear. You're good to stand down."

Over time what we find is that we can make our way to

that shamed part of ourselves that the inner critic was trying to protect, let them know that they are OK and safe now and let go of the shame that was given to us.

Soothe the externalizer

The externalizer deserves your compassion just as much as your inner critic; after all, they are only trying to keep you safe, but they often end up isolating you and hurting other people, so we can't let them carry on as they are. It can be a bit more challenging to catch an externalizer in the moment as it often involves other people, but with time it becomes second nature.

Notice when they rear their head. Are you feeling especially defensive about something? What is going on there?

Pause. We can do this by asking for a minute to process whatever has triggered us. If you're with someone else—perhaps your partner has tried to talk to you about something that has bothered you—you can say, "OK, I hear you. I just need a minute to consider what you've said/think about this/take a breath because it's triggered me and I don't want to respond from that head space." If you're on your own, perhaps reading a text message from a friend to which you want to respond with anger, you might reply: "I'm not ignoring you, but I'm going to take some time to think about what you've said and come back to you when I feel like I'm in a better head space."

Soothe, don't judge. Similar to how we would address an inner critic, here is the point at which we can say to our anger, "Hey, anger, I see you, I know you're here to protect me—I don't need you to do that, I'm safe and I can continue this conversation without becoming defensive. I've got it."

Repair after our protective part has deflected onto someone else is a huge part of our healing journey. We might have to hold ourselves accountable, while letting that part know that we're OK in this moment and we don't have to protect our shamed, vulnerable part.

Understanding the difference between guilt and shame, working with our inner child and shadow, and addressing our different parts are all integral to helping us to step outside of our toxic shame and own all parts of ourselves.

Cycle breaker's toolkit: Is it guilt or is it shame? Or maybe a bit of both?

This is something that I do with clients and it can be really useful for understanding what is ours to hold and what is not.

Take a scenario where you feel what you perceive to be guilt. This could be setting boundaries with a parent (shame), losing your temper with your child over their homework (guilt and shame), forgetting to pick up the ibuprofen your partner needed (guilt) or eating a piece of cake after dinner (shame).

Consider the following:

- What internal messages do I have surrounding this event/ scenario? Where do they come from?
- Did I do something that hurt or impacted others, and how?
- Is this my responsibility? Or within the realm of my control?
- Is this my conscience or lack of self-worth?

Remember:

Shame is something created within you by external messages and it creates feelings of unworthiness. We don't have to have done anything at all for shame to rear its ugly head; it's rooted in our negative self-beliefs.

Guilt is a reasonable reaction to something we have done or said that has caused harm or upset to others and goes against our core values.

If we don't believe we are worthy of setting them and have been taught we are wrong or bad for doing so, we will feel shame about setting boundaries.

If we shout at our child over homework, we will feel guilt at the upset caused because we could have handled the situation differently *and* shame because we have feelings of unworthiness as a parent due to messages given to us as children.

If we forget to pick up the ibuprofen for our partner, we will feel guilty because we have forgotten something that impacts someone else and isn't centered around our self-worth.

If we eat some cake and tell ourselves we need to feel "guilt," that is shame—we haven't got a conscience reaction, we are simply shaming ourselves for enjoying something due to messages given to us either at home or in society about our bodies and food.

Chapter 18

Affirmations

In my opinion, affirmations have become intertwined with "toxic positivity" to a degree—the message we receive is often, "If you're feeling a bit down, just tell yourself in the mirror that you're a boss and you'll be fine . . ." Unfortunately, that's not quite how it works, though it would be lovely if it was. Despite my side-eye to affirmations, I do feel strongly that they can have a place when working with toxic shame or trying to step into a new era in your life. If you struggle with affirmations, that's OK—it doesn't mean that there is anything wrong with you or you're not "getting it," they just might not be for you. I often find it helpful to think of affirmations as speaking to myself with my inner hype woman—she's like the opposite of my inner critic, the angel on my shoulder compared to their devil. I visualize a version of myself who is filled with positive light and kindness as I say affirmations and allow myself to feel warmth wash over me.

Try some of these simple affirmations if you feel able:

- "I am worthy of love, respect and kindness, from myself and others. I know that no matter what I do, I will always be worthy of these things."

- "I do not owe anyone the sacrifice of myself. I am kind and caring—that includes to myself."
- "Other people's reactions to my boundaries are not my responsibility or within my control. I can accept that they may not react how I hope and that doesn't sway me from standing up for myself."
- "I am not a bad person for setting boundaries."
- "I am the parent I needed as a child. I am accountable for my mistakes and I work to be the best parent I can be."
- "I put the work in to heal my wounds because I know I am worthy of that love."
- "My worth is not determined by others."
- "I am good enough just as I am. I don't have to be perfect—my mistakes are lessons I can learn from."

You can add your own affirmations. A tip for working out where we may find an affirmation useful is to consider the areas in which our negative self-talk is most prominent and come up with something that challenges whatever it is we're saying to ourselves without being too confrontational.

Chapter 19

Practicing gratitude

When I used to read about practicing gratitude I always felt the urge to roll my eyes. Like affirmations, it seemed rooted in toxic positivity, with "well, it could be worse" vibes, which is invalidating at the best of times. Would it really be effective in helping me to navigate my experiences and work through challenging situations?

It turns out that practicing gratitude, combined with other supports, can be a great way to help you step out of any drama triangle mindsets, especially if you find yourself falling into the victim role.

My favorite method for practicing gratitude is gratitude journaling. There are plenty of wonderful gratitude journals you can buy, but if you just want a simple practice that you can incorporate into a daily journal, say aloud to yourself while in the shower or even just think on while brushing your teeth or having a morning coffee, then this might be useful for you.

Morning

- **What am I looking forward to today?** This could be anything—going to an event, eating a type of food or drink, watching a TV program, reading a book, seeing your child smile or even just going back to bed. There is no right or wrong way for this to look.
- **What three things am I grateful for in this moment?** Again, this can be anything. The smell of your fabric softener on your clothes, the taste of your morning coffee, the purr of your cat or the fact that your child slept until a certain time. It doesn't matter how small or big these things are or what frustrations surround them. Take a deep breath in and allow yourself to feel the warmth of gratitude. If it doesn't come, that's OK. You're not doing anything wrong, and you don't need to force it.

Evening

- **What are three things that happened today that I'm grateful for?** Don't be afraid to think outside of the box—if you're not feeling particularly positive about your day, this might feel more challenging, and that's OK.

Journaling pages

- What are three things that make you feel loved?

- What would you like your headstone to say and why? This might sound morbid, but often considering a place of finality gives us an idea of what is really important to us.

- Finish this sentence: "My life would be incomplete without . . ."

- What emotions (anger, guilt, embarrassment, happiness, fear) do you find the hardest to accept and why?

- Imagine yourself with no fear, anxiety or shame. You are free and at ease. What would you do with your life without fear?

- If you could imagine your emotions (anger, fear, sadness, joy, etc.) as colors, what colors would they be and why?

- If you could embody your emotions, what or who would they look like? How does that make you feel and what does that bring up for you?

A final note . . .

Congratulations, you've reached the end of this book, but the truth is the work has only just begun and you're never really "done." I'm hoping that by now you're viewing yourself less as a fix-up project and more as a being worthy of self-love, compassion and the effort it takes to go on this healing journey. Yes, your children might be what brought you to this book, but it's important that you leave with a sense that *you* are just as important as they are on this cycle-breaking path. Your journey might have started with them, but I hope it continues with you.

If you've let go of the idea of a perfect parent and dismissed the myth that healing is a yellow brick road with an Emerald City of enlightenment at the end, I've done my job throughout these pages. We can't break cycles and toxic patterns if we're still holding on to those untruths. Healing isn't linear, and while we will break many cycles of generational trauma and toxicity on this path, our children may well have some they want to break too, and that's OK. We can meet them with compassion and support them in ways we likely didn't experience ourselves.

I hope that you feel more accepting of yourself for where you're at now, have a better sense of who you are, flaws and imperfections included, and are aware that life is the project and there is always space for learning and improving. I'm hopeful that you can recognize that breaking cycles is tough, but that every step you take to be the parent you needed, and to hold yourself accountable when you make mistakes and build repairs with your child, *is* cycle breaking at its very core.

Most of all, I'm hopeful that in some way this book has allowed you to recognize how amazing you are, how far you've come and how much effort you are willing to put into being the best version of yourself. It is so much easier to spend life ignoring our generational trauma and refusing to put in the work to heal it, but you made the active choice not to do that, and I think that warrants a celebration of you.

So here's to you, fellow cycle breaker. May you keep growing, learning and being the parent you needed and deserved.

Resources

I felt passionate about including a resources section in the book, in part to underline that we're never "done" with healing and learning to be the best parent we can be, but also to make your life easier, because I know first hand how hard it can be to find the resources you need. I hope this acts as an easy go-to for what to do next.

Further reading
(i.e. the books that have inspired
and helped me on this journey)

For your reparenting journey

Break the Cycle by Dr. Mariel Buqué
Adult Survivors of Emotionally Abusive Parents by Dr. Sherrie
    Campbell
It's Them, Not You by Josh Connolly
It's Not You by Dr. Ramani Durvasula
The Vagus Nerve Reset by Anna Ferguson
Adult Children of Emotionally Immature Parents by Lindsay Gibson
How to Meet Your Self by Dr. Nicole LePera
The Joy of Saying No by Natalie Lue
I'm Glad My Mom Died by Jennette McCurdy
You're Not Crazy—It's Your Mother by Danu Morrigan

This Is How You Grow After Trauma by Dr. Olivia Remes
The Four Tendencies by Gretchen Rubin
No Bad Parts by Richard C. Schwartz
Introduction to Internal Family Systems by Richard C. Schwartz
The Book of Boundaries by Melissa Urban
You're Not the Problem by Helen Villiers and Katie McKenna

For your parenting journey

Calm the Chaos by Dayna Abraham
Raising Good Humans by Hunter Clarke-Fields
Happy Families by Dr. Beth Mosley
There's No Such Thing as "Naughty" by Kate Silverton
Parenting for Humans by Dr. Emma Svanberg
How to Grow a Grown Up by Dr. Dominique Thompson and
   Fabienne Vailes
*How the World Is Making Our Children Mad (and What to Do About
   It)* by Louis Weinstock

Podcasts

Latchkey Urchins & Friends by Alison Cebulla and Anne Sherry
Calling Home with Whitney Goodman
The Therapy Edit with Anna Mathur
Unfollowing Mum by Harriet Shearsmith
In Sight by Helen Villiers and Katie McKenna

Charities and online support networks

Necessary Family Estrangement (run by Sali Hughes), https://www.facebook.com/share/7wy7Cq6VJ8RcH6Kj/?mibextid=K35XfP

StandAlone, www.standalone.org.uk (charity closed in 2024, but the website remains a valuable source of information)

Together Estranged, www.togetherestranged.org

The Village—A Parenting Community for Humans (run by Dr. Emma Svanberg), www.facebook.com/share/pP2Ckb8tQfY2EdyJ/?mibextid=K35XfP

Social media accounts

Instagram

@breakthecycle_coaching
@browngirltherapy
@brownmamatrauma
@cptsd.hope
@dr.sherrie
@doctorramani
@genell.gorman
@helenvilliersma
@josh_ffw
@katiemckennapsychotherapist
@latchkeyurchins
@letsgetyourshifttogether
@maggiewithperspectacles

@manjit_ruprai
@motherwoundproject
@mumologist
@nate_postlethwait
@parent_wound_coach
@responsive_parenting
@sitwithwhit
@thehealingdaughterinc
@the.holistic.psychologist
@tobyandroo
@triinu.co
@unfollowing_mom
@youthemother

TikTok

@fiftiesrediscovery
@healinghumanity777
@rinispencer

Journals

The Big Little Blessings Gratitude Journal from Contoura Collective

The Shadow Work Journal from Zenfulnote

Quizzes

Attachment Style Quiz—a quiz to help you understand and navigate your attachments, www.attachmentproject.com/attachment-style-quiz/

The Four Tendencies quiz—https://gretchenrubin.com/quiz/the-four-tendencies-quiz/

Holistic practice tools

Art therapy ideas for both you and your children (developed by Margaret Naumburg in the 1940s, art therapy is a powerful tool for working on mental health, especially for younger people): www.expressiveartworkshops.com/expressive-art-resources/100-art-therapy-exercises/

Mvmnt app—yoga and Pilates instruction

Sound bath playlist (you will find lots of different versions of this on your chosen listening platform; you can use this during exercises to help you connect to your inner self on a deeper level)

Tibetan bowls playlist (as above, there are studies that show certain sound frequencies create vibrations through the body that have a physiological response and aid stress, tension or help you navigate trauma)

Advice on finding a therapist or coach to work with you after experiencing childhood trauma

Finding a therapist or coach to work with after you have experienced childhood trauma can be challenging. What a lot of people don't realize is that therapy isn't a one-size-fits-all thing and sometimes, like jeans in a boutique store, we have to try on a few different sizes and brands until we find the right one. Given that there are hundreds of therapeutic approaches and different skill levels and experiences within each, it can feel like a minefield, but I've put together some advice below to help you work out where to start.

Notable therapeutic approaches you may wish to consider

The following are therapeutic approaches that are specifically recommended for trauma survivors, but I would like to note that many therapists will consider themselves "integrative therapists," which means they blend approaches to best suit their clients. Please don't discount a therapist who doesn't use these approaches but can offer you trauma-led therapy.

Eye Movement Desensitisation Reprocessing (EMDR)

According to the American Psychological Association (APA), EMDR is "a structured therapy that encourages the patient to briefly focus on the trauma memory while simultaneously experiencing bilateral stimulation (typically eye movements), which is associated with a reduction in the vividness and emotion associated with the trauma memories." EMDR works off the adaptive processing theory of how our brain stores memories, and specifically focuses on changing the emotions, thoughts and feelings that arise from traumatic events.

Emotional freedom technique (EFT)

This is sometimes referred to as "tapping" and involves tapping meridian points while you focus on a particular memory or experience. It's often referred to as "acupuncture for the mind, without needles!" and receives high praise from CPTSD, PTSD and trauma communities.

Cognitive behavioral therapy (CBT)

CBT is a type of talk therapy that challenges your beliefs about yourself. While this might be effective for some people, CBT is often criticized for being ineffective for developmental trauma and lacking in trauma-informed practice. However, it is still one of the most commonly used/recommended therapies for dealing with PTSD.

What to ask a potential therapist or coach:

- Are you a trauma-informed therapist?
- Do you have experience working with people who have experienced developmental/childhood trauma?
- How would you best approach working with me on that?
- What can I expect from working with you?

Other things to consider/ask:

- What qualifications do you hold?
- What regulatory body are you registered with?
- What length of time do you think we need to work together for, how many sessions and will we review?

Acknowledgments

I'd like to thank the team at Ebury publishing for guiding me through this process—writing a book might look like a solo project but it's far from it. Not unlike parenting, it takes a village, and I'm so grateful for the support and advice at every stage. In particular, my editor, Anya—this book wouldn't be here if she hadn't believed in me and the need for something like this in the world. Thank you.

Craig Knox for believing in me and fighting to make this happen. Your endless support means the world and I know you're always by my side.

My clients and those who have entrusted me to coach them through estrangement and healing—you teach me every day and it will continue to be one of my greatest honors to be a part of your healing journey.

My online community, I am so incredibly proud of the space we have created together. From the podcast, which is filled with lived experiences and professional support, to the social media communities we have forged together. This space was *needed*. It was my wish to create a space that would let someone who was in the position I was when I first cut contact with my mom know that they aren't alone. We did that.

Finally, and most importantly, my children. I know I won't

break every cycle. I will make mistakes along the way and we will have to have some tough conversations, but I hope, with every fiber of my being, you know that I love you. Everything I do, I do with you in my heart. You will be forever etched onto my soul and I will never stop striving to be better for you.

About the Author

Born in Yorkshire, **Harriet Shearsmith** is a certified coach, trainee therapist and award-winning content creator. She is one of the most prominent professional parenting voices in the UK. With a focus on cycle-breaking parenting, she helps other parents to be the parent they wish they'd had as they heal their generational trauma. Harriet has created a podcast, *Unfollowing Mum*, and online community supporting adult children of dysfunctional, toxic families and discusses topics from estrangement to healing childhood wounds.

Hi there,

We hope *Cycle Breakers* helped you. If you have any questions or concerns about your book, or have received a damaged copy, please contact customerservice@penguinrandomhouse.com. We're here and happy to help.

Also, please consider writing a review on your favorite retailer's website to let others know what you thought of the book.

Sincerely,
The Zeitgeist Team